D1145152

Malmesbury Lace

Malmesbury Lace

Joan Blanchard

B.T. Batsford Limited · London

The jacket illustrations show *front*: Malmesbury Market Cross
and *back*: Malmesbury Lacemaking School *c.* 1909.

First published 1990
© Joan Blanchard 1990

All rights reserved. No part of this publication may be reproduced,
in any form or by any means,
without permission from the Publisher

ISBN 0 7134 6615 4

Typeset by
Lasertext Ltd.
And printed by
The Bath Press, Bath

For the publisher
B. T. Batsford Limited
4 Fitzhardinge Street
London W1H 0AH

Contents

Reference Information

author's adaptation of original pattern

Foreword

I started teaching lacemaking in 1983. One of my first students asked me if I knew anything about Malmesbury lace. I had to admit I did not, and promptly set about getting some information on the subject. I visited the Athelstan Museum in Malmesbury and met the Curator, Mrs Prince, who has been most helpful, and over the years since then we have become good friends. She gave me the name of another lady, Mrs Glenna Paynter, who had been born in Malmesbury but now lived in Wales. In answer to a letter, this lady wrote about the lace school which her aunt had attended in about 1910. She also wrote that her information would need to be checked, 'should I be thinking of publishing'. This was like a challenge to me, and slowly I gathered more information, making numerous visits to Trowbridge Record Office and the Museum, where I made diagrams of the lace on display and made new patterns and new samples – the patterns in the museum are so badly worn they cannot be used to produce a good piece of lace any more.

Gradually I was introduced to more and more people who had connections with the lace school, often because their mothers attended. One, Mrs Gertrude Farrar, was there herself in 1913, as a child of six and was able to give me some details. She may well be the only surviving member of those classes. The whole subject became like a huge jigsaw puzzle with pieces dropping into place bit by bit.

I have many other people to thank for their help and encouragement over the past five years: Mrs Grace Lee, my first lace tutor; Miss Doreen Campbell, who introduced me to Miss Dorothy Barnes, who has been most generous in lending me samples and prickings; Chippenham Library Staff; North Wiltshire County Council; Trowbridge Record Office Staff; Pamela Colman, Librarian at the Wiltshire Archeological and Natural History Society; Mrs Mary Gibson at the Salisbury and South Wiltshire Museum; the staff at Bristol Reference Library; Miss Pamela Clark, Assistant Registrar at the Royal Archives, Windsor; Richard Needham, MP; Betty McInnes at the House of Commons Library; S. K. Ellison at the House of Lords Record Office; staff at the Public Record Office, London and Kew; Sue Stork for typing my historical script; June Tiley for typing pattern instructions; and Mr Eric Pascoe, photographer, BA, ABIPP. Also Mrs Susanne Thompson, who helped me with techniques for making the Malmesbury Market Cross lace.

Part One

The Background

The Early Years

Malmesbury is an ancient town, standing on a hilltop, close to the county border in north-west Wiltshire. Approached from the south, the Abbey stands out above the town. It took over 200 years to build, and it became a seat of learning with a great library. It was completed in 1460, but less than 100 years later, in 1539, came the Dissolution of the Monasteries, when it was partly ruined. Leland, the historian, passed through the town in about 1543, and wrote that the Abbey, though ruined, was still standing, and the houses of office (such as the refectory) were filled with looms for weaving. Three thousand cloths (each about 24 m (27 yds) long, 160 cm (5 ft) broad and weighing about 17 kg (44 lbs)) were made in the town every year. Leland also remarked upon the fine Market Cross, which dates from 1490. One assumes that, had he seen lace being made while in Malmesbury, he surely would have mentioned it.

The earliest record of lace in this area is found in Mrs Bury Palliser's *A History of Lace*, and in James Waylen's *History of Marlborough* (1853). During the Civil War (1642–1648) Sir Edward Hungerford's soldiers attacked Wardour Castle, near Shaftesbury. Lady Arundel, who lived there, described the destruction and stated that the soldiers cut up the lead pipe and sold it, 'as these men's wives, in North Wiltshire, do bonelace and sell it at six pence a yard'.

Mrs Bury Palliser also mentions seaming and spacing lace being used in the seventeenth century to join widths of fabric, instead of just sewing a seam. The first five patterns in this book would have been most suitable for this purpose.

Later in Waylen's *History of Marlborough* there is a reference to the Great Plague of 1665, with specific mention of certain people in the town, one who had died of the plague and others who had been in contact with her. These people were ordered to remain shut up in their

Map of Wiltshire, showing Malmesbury and surrounding towns

● Crudwell

● Brokenborough

● Hankerton

● Charlton ● Minety

● MALMESBURY

● Corston

● CHIPPENHAM

● MARLBOROUGH

● BRADFORD-ON-AVON

● DEVIZES

● TROWBRIDGE

WILTSHIRE

● SALISBURY

● Downton

● Morgans Vale

● Redlynch

houses: 'all parents and masters should be cautious in sending their children and servants to school, in making bonelace or otherwise'. So we can conclude that there was at least one lace school in Marlborough at that time.

That reference to lace schools makes sense of another record. In Trowbridge Record Office, there is an entry in the Marlborough Parish Register for the burial of the wife of Simon Hurl, in 1670; Simon died a year later. So, in 1671, their daughter Mary, now an orphan aged eight, was apprenticed by the Mayor and Councillors to Walter Martyn, a butcher, to be instructed and employed in the art of bonelace making. Her sister, Joane Hurl, was also apprenticed, to John Miles, husbandman (probably meaning farmer), again to be instructed in the art of bonelace making. Both girls were also to be instructed in housewifery and domestic employment. The fact that the two girls were not apprenticed to actual lacemakers in order to learn to make lace may seem rather curious (although of course it is possible that the wives of the two men were lacemakers), but consider Waylen's mention of lace schools. There children were taught to read and write, and also to make lace. Mary certainly had an education, for later she wrote an account of her conversion to Christianity, which was published in 1719, and can now be found in the Bodleian Library in Oxford. Unfortunately, she does not specifically mention the lace she made, although she does say that a 'Religious Man' called at the house one day, and 'I listened as I sat at my work', which could well have referred to her lacemaking.

The only other reference to Mary's Apprenticeship Deed appears in a chapter in the *Wiltshire Archaeological Magazine* of 1671. She was apprenticed to Walter Martyn for eight years and says she then apprenticed herself at another place for five. She then went to live with an aunt.

The Dutch and French influence

In E. Lipson's *Economic History of England*, he states that in 1672 Charles II issued a Declaration inviting Dutch artisans to settle in England. In response, a number of families came over, merchants, skippers with their vessels, at least

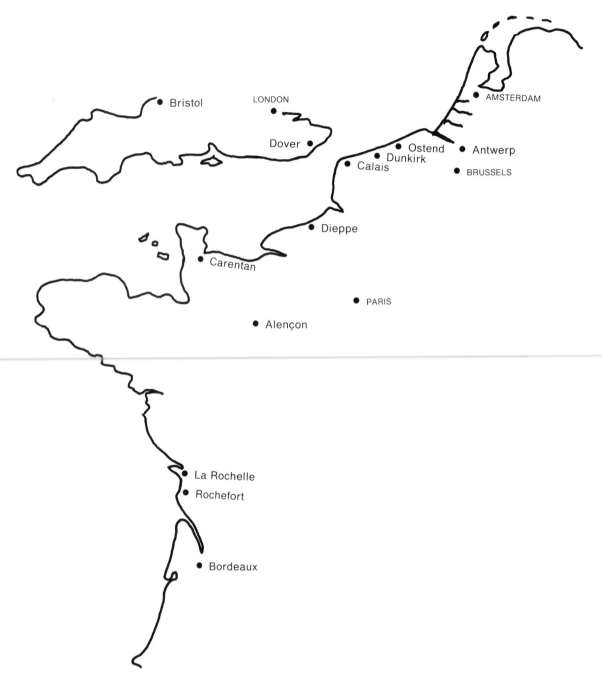

Map of part of Northern Europe, showing places where lacemakers may have come from

one porcelain tile maker, and most importantly, weavers.
Many of them settled in Wiltshire, especially in and
around Trowbridge. The following appears in the Privy
Council Register, in the Public Record Office in London:

> *At the Court at Whitehall*
> *May 9th 1673*
> ...certain Dutchmen skilled in the art of weaving fine
> cloth, to the number of twenty three and about fifteen
> persons...have been recommended to the care of Mr
> William Brewer of Trowbridge in Wiltshire, a clothier,
> unto which place the said persons are all now removing
> in order to set forward and promote their knowledge
> and skill in the making of cloth.

Malmesbury was noted for its weaving (Leland gave
detailed comments on it), and many of these weavers could
have moved to Malmesbury. While there seem to be no
Settlement Certificates for them, names such as Plurott,
Gryst, Vonoll, Burquis, Voote, Sarbort, Grayle, Bohun and
Blanchot appear in Bradford-on-Avon and Malmesbury
registers at this time.

Although the earlier records prove otherwise, the oral
tradition is that the Dutch immigrants introduced the craft
of lacemaking to Wiltshire. Certainly the Dutch settlement
had a profound, and refining, influence on English bonelace
making. It is more than likely that many of the weavers'
wives were lacemakers. In early records, wives' occupations
are not usually listed, but as is illustrated in the Bristol
register discussed later in this chapter, those of single
women and widows often are. A great many of the widows
on the register are lacemakers.

The refining influence of Dutch lacemaking is apparent in a
comment made in 1680 by the historian John Aubrey, who
was born between Chippenham and Castle Combe: 'Our
Shepherdesses do begin to make point lace, whereas, before
the Civil War they only knitted course stockings' (*Natural
History of Wiltshire*, ed. J. Britten, 1847).

In 1681 there was an influx into the area of French
Protestant refugees, known as Huguenots. Several hundreds
settled in Bristol. In Vol. XLIX of the *Huguenot Society
Quarto Series*, we see that for the Relief of French
Protestant Refugees 1681–87, a National Fund had been
administered from London. Among many others who were

given money for shoes, clothing, bedding and food were the following names of some lacemakers.

Marie Debie, a widow with a daughter aged 20
Madeleine Menanteau from Paris and Charenton
Jacques Monnoy from Paris
Jean Page from Rennes
Francois Parisot
Isaac Perie with a wife and 3 children
Marie Barbée a widow from Dieppe
Marie Berville a widow from Dieppe
Thomas Perier from Alençon, with a wife and daughter
aged 7, lacemaker and linen weaver

The names were in three sections, the first headed 'Faiseuse de Dentelle', the second, 'Bonelace' and the third, 'Point lace'. Thomas Perier is of particular interest as he combined the trades of weaver and lacemaker. Also note the fact that many of the lacemakers who received relief were widows. Rarely could they support themselves by lacemaking alone. For them the trade seems to have been a means of making just a little extra money.

As for Malmesbury itself, there are various records, including, in the Malmesbury Parish Register of 1698, that of the burial of a child of Mary Punter, bonelace maker. Again, in 1700, there is a record of the burial of Elizabeth Jones, lacemaker, at Malmesbury. In 1701 there is an entry in the same register for the burial of Thomas Hestour, laceman.

From Lace to Silk

In 1793 Mr Hill, of Bradford-on-Avon, bought the old
Cannop's Mill by St John's Bridge over the River Avon,
south of the town. He added another building and opened
a cloth factory. In evidence at a Select Committee on the
Woollen Trade in 1795, Malmesbury inhabitants said they

*Malmesbury Lacemaking School, The Kings Arms, High Street,
c. 1909. (From left to right) Back row: Elsie Vaughan, Florrie
Bishop, Annie Bishop, May Jacobs, May Tanner; Middle row:
Florrie Weeks, Ms Denley, Mrs Jones (proprietress King's
Arms), Mrs Fisher (tutor), Florrie Drew, Cassie Drew; Bottom
row: Daisy Jefferies, Hilda Fry, Maud Phelps, Nell Jefferies,
May Reeves, Eva Jefferies, Kitty Bond*

could earn more by lacemaking than by working at the factory – the best laceworkers were getting 8/- to 10/- a week (40p–50p).

However, after 1763, when Morris first made a lacy fabric on the stocking machine, other people began to invent or adapt lace machines, among them Hammond, Rogers and Heathcoat. The last-mentioned patented a machine in 1808 which made lace 2.5 cm (1 in) wide. A year later he patented a second machine which made lace of any width. Due to these machines, by 1826 the hand lace industry was declining, and a report states that even the best lacemakers could earn no more than 2/6 to 3/- a week ($12\frac{1}{2}$p to 15p) at Malmesbury.

In 1830 Cannop's Mill changed hands, and Mr Salter of Kington Langley owned it for about 20 years. In 1852 it was taken over by Bridget Thomas and Co., and it became a silk mill. It changed hands again in 1855, but continued as a silk mill.

By comparing the censuses taken from 1841–1851, it is evident that many women and girls gave up lacemaking to work in the silk mill. No doubt they could earn more there. The figures for these years are:

1841	96 adult lacemakers
1851	150 adult lacemakers
1861	49 adult lacemakers
1871	17 adult lacemakers
1881	11 adult lacemakers

By contrast, research by Malmesbury schoolchildren (*Man in Malmesbury*) shows that by 1862 there were 280 workers at the silk mill, although some of these were children who worked half a day in the mill and went to school for half a day.

Lacemaking was not only declining in Malmesbury. According to the Census taken in Marlborough in 1851, there was just one lacemaker, a Martha Bajust, aged 32. But she was born at Amersham, Buckinghamshire, and so quite possibly she learnt the craft before she ever arrived at Marlborough. It is not surprising that lacemaking had died out in that town. It is on the main London-to-Bath road, a very busy route, and there must have been plenty of other work available there, in the inns, for example.

Similarly, the 1851 Census for Devizes shows that by then there was a silk mill in this town too, which employed over 80 people. Again, just one lacemaker is listed in the town, Elizabeth Langley, aged 21. She lived at Devizes Green and was born at Malmesbury.

Interestingly, a John Donnel, aged 34, is also listed, as a lace hawker. He was born in Ireland and seems to have moved about frequently. His children were born at Bristol, Marlborough and Devizes. Could he have been a 'middle man' between Malmesbury and Salisbury, where there was at least one lace dealer and two lacemakers? All the other lacemakers on the Census lived in the Downton and Redlynch areas.

The only place where lacemaking seemed to be occurring on any sort of scale in the mid-nineteenth century was in the Bethlehem Hospital, which must have been the Workhouse. It had 156 inmates, according to the *Salisbury and Winchester Journal* of 1841, 108 of whom were employed in various crafts, including lacemaking. Meanwhile, the records of Malmesbury Workhouse do not mention any attempt to teach lacemaking.

As lacemaking declined in the area, so, presumably, did the popularity of lace, leading to surplus stock. In the *Salisbury and Winchester Journal* the following item appeared:

> In the lace trade at Chard, steady employment is afforded to the hands, but master manufacturers complain of slow demand and accumulating stock.

Perhaps for the same reason the following notice also appeared in the newspaper that year:

> Notice to the Ladies of Salisbury.
> Mr H. Hales, British and Foreign Lace Warehouse
>   22 High Street, Southampton
> Mr Hale has arranged with Mr Jones of the White Hart Hotel to have a room from which to sell lace – Mechlin, Valenciennes, Point de Paris, Antwerp, Lille, Pillow, Isle of Wight. The sale will take place on November 1st, 2nd and 3rd.

Lacemaking was still going on in the schools
(for instance, in the 1859 Census for Wiltshire schools,
The Abbey School in the Parish is recorded as having an

assistant mistress teaching lace) but it was fast dying out even there. There was a 'Ragged School' in Burnivale, Malmesbury, which eventually closed in 1886. The average number of children attending had been 115, but while pens, pencils, needles and thimbles were kept in store and sold to the children, there is no mention of lacemaking being taught. By early this century, lacemaking in school seems to be history. A newspaper item in Malmesbury Museum, dated 1908, states that 'Seventy years ago (1838) lacemaking was taught in the Dame School. Boys and girls alike had to take a turn at the bobbins and pillow. The children commenced at five years'.

We have already seen the figures for adult lacemakers in Malmesbury from 1841 to 1881. In the Malmesbury Census of 1841, there were five children (girls under 12, boys under 14) listed as lacemakers; in 1851, there were 46; but by 1861, there were none. However, there were five child silkworkers. There were no children listed as lacemakers in 1871 or 1881 and by this time, there were only 11 adults. By 1900, only six were left.

Revival and Survival

In 1904 the Earl of Suffolk, who lived at Charlton Park, near Malmesbury, married Marguerite Hyde, daughter of the late Levi Leiter of Washington, U.S.A. Realising that the lacemaking craft might die out, she set about organizing a lace school, which started in 1907. It was held in the Market Room of the Kings Arms Hotel, in Malmesbury High Street.

The class was held once a week for one hour and children and young women came from a wide area. Censuses taken at the time give names of lacemakers from as far away as Hankerton, Corston, Crudwell, Lea and Brokenborough, all villages surrounding the town.

There is a newspaper report stating that the Countess also had a stall at the *Dail Mail* 'Exhibition of British Lace' in 1908. At that time there were 30 pupils, with more waiting to join, and two teachers, one old, one young, but it does not give their names. (It is this newspaper report which mentions children at the Dame School, 70 years previously, making lace, and also gives the names of some lace patterns. Another newspaper report dated January 27th, 1912, from the *Wiltshire Times*, gives a report about the lace school, some more names of patterns, and states that orders had come from as far afield as America, Germany, Egypt and India.

Lady Suffolk provided the pillows and bobbins for the school, but one of the first pupils, Annie Goodfield, née Bishop, found the pillows too soft, and took her grandmother's pillow to class instead. Her grandmother urged her not to let lacemaking die out in Malmesbury. Annie became an excellent lacemaker and won a cup for her expertise. In 1912 she helped to make lace for the trousseau of Princess Alexandra, daughter of the Princess Royal.

At the age of 13, Annie had to go into service and there was no time for lacemaking. Many years later, in 1968,

Malmesbury held a Festival of Flowers and Annie was persuaded to get out her pillow and demonstrate the craft. 'Annie's Pattern' (Pattern 13 in this book) is the one she is seen making in a photograph. There is a painting of her in the museum, dressed in the costume she wore at the festival. Annie died in 1981, just before I started my research.

Lizzie Barnes (née White) also attended the lace school in 1909. At the Malmesbury Flower Show that year she won first prize in the under 12 years lacemaking class (the prize was 5/- (25p) and a certificate) and continued to win prizes

Lizzie Barnes (née White) c. 1911

for years to come. Over this time, the patterns she made included 'The Egg', 'The Diamond', 'Cat's Eye', 'Clover Leaf', 'Narrow Baby Lace' (which is either Pattern 1 or Pattern 2 in Part Two), and 'The Allotment'. We do not know precisely which pattern 'The Allotment' represents, but its name may come from the allotments of land which each of the commoners held – in AD 939 King Athelstan had given the Common of Malmesbury to the descendants of the men who fought for him in the battle. (During World War II, the land was ploughed, and the commoners now receive rent in lieu of their allotments).

Lizzie kept a notebook on the amount of lace she made. The largest piece, which seems to have been 25/27 yards (23/25 metres) long, was cut off and sold for £12. Other amounts earned were between 1/- and 11/- (5p and 55p). She bought her thread from Hodders, in the High Street. An idea of prices for her materials at that time can be gleaned from receipts in her scrap book. One, dated 1931, is for a hank of lace thread at 2/- (10p). She also bought

Lizzie Barnes (right), with her daughter Dorothy (left)

goods by post from Jonathan Harris and Sons, Derwent Mills, Cockermouth, Cumberland (now Cumbria). Pure flax thread was priced $11\frac{1}{2}$ d to 4/2 (5p to 21p). A large Bruges mushroom pillow cost 12/6 ($62\frac{1}{2}$p), a small one cost 6/6 ($32\frac{1}{2}$p). Bobbins were 1/3 to 2/3 ($6\frac{1}{2}$p to $11\frac{1}{2}$p) per dozen. Old bobbins with names were 3 d to 3/6 ($1\frac{1}{2}$p to $17\frac{1}{2}$p). A Harris Torchon Lace book with illustrations cost 6 d ($2\frac{1}{2}$p). There was no date on the price lists but receipts were dated 1923, 1931 and 1932.

I have not been able to establish the date when the lace school finished – it may have been early in the World War 1. But sometime in the 1920s when the Kings Arms Hotel changed hands, all the remaining patterns were sold, and Mrs Barnes bought some of them.

In her scrap book there is a letter dated 1937 from Miss Edith Glyn of Landford Manor, Salisbury, which reads:

Lacemaking in Malmesbury Museum, 1987 (courtesy of Evening Advertiser/Wiltshire Gazette and Herald)

Dear Mrs Barnes

I am returning the parchments and samples you lent me. I have copied 12 of them, some from the parchments and some from the lace itself.

These 12 patterns were entered in the Downton Record Books as 'Patterns 137–151, Malmesbury Lace'. Some had names. The Downton Records are now held at Trowbridge Record Office.

In the early 1930s, Miss Dorothy Barnes was taught at the age of seven, by her mother, to make lace. She sold some of her lace through the Downton Lace Industry, sending it by post to Salisbury and receiving payment by post. Over the years, Dorothy has taught several local people to make lace and has written down some instructions for patterns. She herself was taught by word of mouth, but although her mother was scornful of her writing down the instructions, they have enabled me to establish that Malmesbury lace is made in the same way as Bucks Point (see next section for characteristics of Malmesbury lace). Note that I have not included any of those patterns here which I have seen reproduced in other books.

During one of my many visits to Malmesbury Museum, Mrs Prince, the Curator, asked me to put on a demonstration of lacemaking, so in 1987, Doreen Campbell, a lace tutor in Malmesbury, a student of hers, Rosemary Exton, and myself, spent a day in the museum making lace, and we had many interested visitors. Since then, Rosemary and sometimes Doreen too, have been demonstrating regularly.

Hopefully, with the help of this book and these demonstrations, the interest which people are showing in Malmesbury lace will continue to grow, and the craft will not die out completely, as was once nearly the case.

Malmesbury Lace

Malmesbury Museum is well-furnished with artefacts relating the history of its lace, including an incomplete bobbin winder, which was used by a Mrs Trotman in about 1830. At this time thread was bought in hanks, as was knitting wool. Hodders, in the High Street, was the place to buy lace thread. The hank was stretched around the adjustable pegs on the four arms, and as the wheel was turned the thread could be wound on to the bobbin. There is also a gadget like a cotton reel on a wooden handle. This was a much simpler winder, the thread being wound on to the cotton reel from the hank, then from it on to the bobbin. Recently, I have seen more of these winders, which were specially made with a tapering handle which fits into a tapered hole in the cotton reel.

The traditional Malmesbury bobbins were, like those at Downton, unspangled. This is because the thread used was very fine, and the weight of spangles would have snapped the thread. However, whereas the Downton bobbins are tapered and some have pictures of birds on them (could the bird be meant to represent the almost extinct bustard, which used to breed in Wiltshire, or a cuckoo, since Downton has a Cuckoo Fair each year?), the Malmesbury bobbins are straight and plain, with a flat end. Although there are some in the Museum with pewter rings, these were not the true Malmesbury bobbins.

The pillow in the Museum, on a bow fronted 'pillow horse', is one of many still in the town. Most of them are now kept as mementoes, but one or two are still used. Each is like a huge football, and quite round.

A pattern was then called a 'parchment' and it had fabric ends stitched on to it which were pinned to the pillow. This was called a 'peel'. When a worker reached the bottom of the pattern, all the bobbins were wrapped in the cover cloth, the pins were removed and the lace was carefully lifted, supporting the bobbins, to the top of the

Malmesbury lacemaker, date unknown. Note the football shape of the pillow and the plainness of the bobbins

pattern again. The thick, outlining thread, which we now call gimp, was called bunting. Passive threads were called straight cottons, and tallies were known as basket filling.

Parchment is mentioned in a letter which can be seen in the museum, dated May 8th 1903. It reads:

Dear Miss Rachel,
Mrs White brought the enclosed patterns of lace this morning and asked me to let you have them, also the

parchment which you have promised to try to get pricked for her. She wishes me to say that she would like to have the old pattern back with the new one, as then if there is anything wrong in the new one, she could alter it with the old one to go by.

The names for the lace she sent are Mignonette, the wide one, Small fan, the narrow, and Footing, the insertion.

Louie Hanks.

Malmesbury lace seems to have been used mainly for cuffs and edgings. Pieces of the lace itself are on display in the museum, and include a collar and a baby's bonnet, with lace edge and insert. Malmesbury lace would certainly be most attractive in the yoke of a christening gown. Perhaps this helps give rise to the intriguing legend that in 1841 Malmesbury and Downton lacemakers met at Devizes to make lace for the layette of Queen Victoria's second child. Wiltshire lacemakers did gather together at that time, according to Miss Glyn's *Downton Lace Booklet* and other records of the industry – but there is no positive proof in the royal archives at Windsor Castle that the layette ever existed. (Unless, of course, anyone knows better.)

Characteristics of Malmesbury Lace

As we have seen, Malmesbury lace has been made for at least three centuries in the town, but no very early samples survive, so it is impossible to tell exactly what it was like at its beginnings.

Today, Malmesbury lace is similar to Downton. Originally it may not have been, judging by the differences in the shape of the bobbins (as we have seen from the examples in the museum) and in the style of the pillows, Downton's being roller pillows and Malmesbury's very round, and larger than Honiton's. Also, Downton workers have their footside on the left, while Malmesbury workers have theirs on the right.

Communication between Downton and Malmesbury seems to have been carried out from the introduction of the Penny Post in 1840, and so perhaps the similarities between their laces began to be reinforced at that time.

Malmesbury lacemaker, date unknown. Note the extreme fineness of the threads used in the lace

If the legend about the layette for Queen Victoria's child has any truth in it, then surely the lacemaking techniques must have been compatible. Certainly both laces use Bucks Point techniques, and both can be distinguished from it by the fineness of their threads (as fine as Honiton), which means that neither needs the weight of spangles.

Although many patterns were exchanged between Downton and Malmesbury, there are a few which I have not been able to find outside Malmesbury, such as Flemish Centre Braid, Ladder Braid, Little Diamond and Clover Leaf (Pattern numbers 1, 2, 5 and 17 in this book). Also exclusive to Malmesbury, as far as I can tell, are the irregular chevron on Chain and Whole Stitch Chevron (Pattern 12) and the fan found on 'Annie's Pattern' and Fan and Chain (Pattern numbers 13 and 14).

Malmesbury lace itself is a very fine geometric lace made at angles varying between 52 and 60 degrees. My samples are made at 1/13 – 13 holes to the inch (2.5 cm) along the footside – but many patterns were made on a finer grid. Identical patterns may have been made elsewhere, but

Amy Wilkins

many are unique. Most are geometric, but a few, such as Clover Leaf, have Floral Bucks techniques.

The narrowest Malmesbury lace is only a quarter of an inch (seven millimetres) wide, and may have been used for joining wider pieces of lace together or for joining two pieces of fabric. The narrow pieces to be found in this book form a good introduction to the working of Malmesbury lace.

A note on threads

The thread generally used for Malmesbury lace was as fine as Honiton: 140–180 in Brok cotton. Most of the samples in this book have been worked in DMC Brillante 50, though Retors d'Alsace and Brok 100 are of similar thickness. Both Brillante and Retors d'Alsace are now marketed under the name 'Broder Machine'.

Hints on making Malmesbury lace

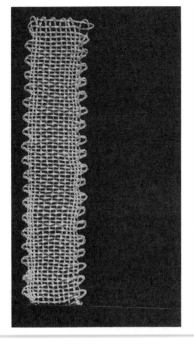
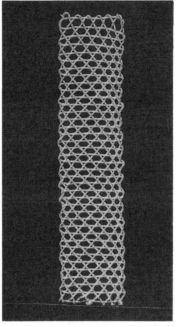
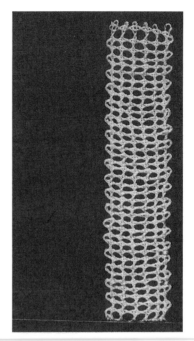

*Whole
Stitch
(Cloth
Stitch)
(W.S)*

*Half
Stitch
($\frac{1}{2}$ St)*

*Whole
Stitch
Twist
(W.S.Tw)*

Number the bobbins from the left 1, 2, 3, 4.
Start by placing 2 over 3. Mentally renumber the bobbins and simultaneously place 2 over 1 and 4 over 3. Again mentally renumber the bobbins and place 2 over 3. This is a complete whole stitch.

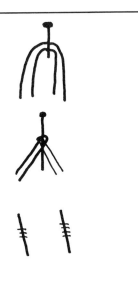

Hanging pairs 'open' or splayed around a pin.

Hanging pairs side by side around a pin.

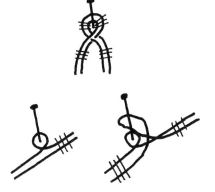

Lines denote the number of twists on a pair. A twist is made by placing right bobbin over left as at 4 over 3.

False Picot. Hang 2 pairs open. Twist 3 on each. Whole stitch twist 3 on each.

Picot on the Left. Twist 3. Hold a pin with the point towards you and from the left pass it under and over the left thread and into the pin hole. Keep the thread slack. Pass the 2nd thread round the pin clockwise. Twist 3, open out the pair to ease the twists up to the pin.

Reverse for a picot on the right.

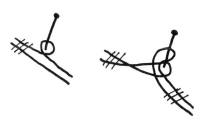

i.e. Twist 3. Hold a pin with the point towards you and from the right pass it under and over the right thread and into the pin hole. Keep the thread slack. Pass the 2nd thread round the pin anticlockwise. Twist 3, open out the pair to ease the twists up to the pin.

Part Two

The Patterns

Pattern 1:
Flemish Centre Braid

Bobbins   6 pairs

Hang 2 pairs open on left pin. Hang 2 pairs open on right
pin. Hang 1 pair on each pin inside.

*W.S. Tw 3 with 2 pairs on left. Give left pair 1 more Tw
and leave. With right pair W.S. through 1 pair Tw 3
and leave. W.S. Tw 3 with 2 pairs on right. Give right
pair 1 more Tw and leave. With left pair W.S. through
1 pair Tw 3. W.S. Tw 3 with the two centre pairs, put up
centre pin. W.S. Tw 3. W.S. through 1 pair each with
those 2 centre pairs, Tw 3 and put up the edge pin.

Repeat from *.

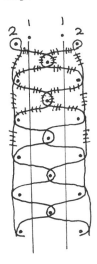

Diagram 1. *Flemish Centre
Braid*

Pricking 1.
*Flemish
Centre Braid*

1. *Flemish
Centre Braid*

Pattern 2:
Ladder Braid

Bobbins   8 pairs

Hang 2 pairs open on left pin. Hang 2 pairs open on right pin. Hang 2 pairs on each pin inside.

*W.S. Tw 3 with 2 left hand pairs. Give edge pair 1 more Tw and leave. With right hand pair of these 2, W.S. through 2 pairs, Tw 3 and leave. With the 2 right hand pairs W.S. Tw 3. Give the edge pair 1 more Tw and leave. With left hand pair W.S. through 2 pairs, Tw 3.

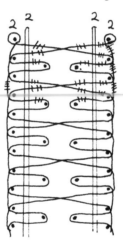

2. *Ladder Braid*

W.S. Tw 3 with the 2 centre pairs. **No pin at centre.** The 'workers' will have changed sides. With left hand of these 2 pairs, W.S. through 2 pairs, Tw 3 and put up edge pin.

W.S. with 2 left hand pairs. Give edge pair 1 more Tw and leave. With right hand of these 2 pairs, W.S. through 2 pairs, Tw 3 and put up inside pin. W.S. back through 2 pairs, Tw 3, put up edge pin and leave.

Diagram 2. *Ladder Braid*

With the new right hand worker, W.S. through 2 pairs, Tw 3, put up edge pin. W.S. Tw 3 with the 2 right hand pairs. Give the edge pair 1 more Tw and leave. With left hand of these 2 pairs, W.S. through 2 pairs, Tw 3, put up inside pin. W.S. back through 2 pairs, Tw 3, put up edge pin.

Repeat from *.

Pricking 2. *Ladder Braid*

Pattern 3:
Basket Filling

Bobbins   8 pairs

Hang 2 pairs of bobbins open at right and left and 2 pairs on temporary pins inside each.

W.S. Tw 3, with the 2 pairs at left. Give the edge pair 1 more Tw and leave. With the right hand pair, W.S. through 2 pairs, Tw 2, put up pin A. W.S. back through 2 pairs. Tw 3, put up pin **B**. W.S. Tw 3 with the edge pair. Give the edge pair 1 more Tw and W.S. back through the 2 pairs with the right hand pair. Tw 2 and leave all these pairs.

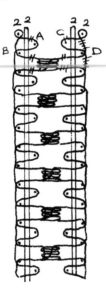

Diagram 3a. *Basket Filling*

With the 2 pairs at the right, W.S. Tw 3, give the edge pair 1 more TW and leave. With the left hand pair W.S. through 2 pairs, Tw 2, put up pin **C**. W.S. back through 2 pairs, Tw 3, put up pin **D**. W.S. Tw 3 with the edge pair, give the edge pair 1 more Tw and leave. With the left hand pair, W.S. through 2 pairs, Tw 2.

With this pair and the pair to its left, a basket filling, or tally, is made by weaving one of the four threads over and under the other three. Basket filling is the old Malmesbury name for these little tallies.

On page 14 of *A Visual Introduction to Bucks Point Lace* by Geraldine Stott (Batsford), she gives diagrams for three possible ways of working these, suggesting that the worker should try them all and use the method she likes best.

3. *Basket Filling*

Pattern 4:
The Egg

Bobbins   8 pairs – Gimps   2 pairs

Hang the 2 pairs of gimps on a temporary pin at the centre, splayed one outside the other. Hang 2 pairs of bobbins side by side on the pins to the right and left. Hang 2 more pairs of bobbins on each outside pin, splayed.

W.S. Tw 3 with 2 pairs on left. With right of these, W.S. through 2 pairs, Tw 3 and W.S. through the 2 left gimps, using the gimps as a pair of threads, Tw the workers twice, and put up pin at **A**. W.S. back through the gimp pair, Tw 3, W.S. through 2 pairs, Tw 3, and put up edge pin at **B**. W.S. Tw 3 with the edge pair, give the left hand pair 1 more Tw, and leave.

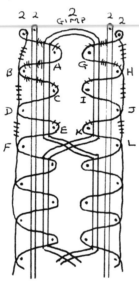

Diagram 4. *The Egg*

*W.S. through 2 pairs, Tw 3, W.S. through the gimp pair, Tw twice, and put up pin **C**. W.S. back through the gimp pair, Tw 3, W.S. through 2 pairs, Tw 3, and put up the edge pin at **D**. W.S. Tw 3 with the edge pair, and give the edge pair 1 more Tw.

Repeat from *, putting up a pin at **E** and another at **F**. Leave.

W.S. Tw 3 with the 2 right hand pairs, and give the edge pair 1 more TW. With the left hand pair, W.S. through 2 pairs, Tw 3, W.S. through the 2 right hand gimps, Tw 2, and put up pin at **G. W.S. through the gimp pair, Tw 3, whole stitch through 2 pairs, Tw 3, and put up the edge pin at **H**.

Repeat from **, putting up pins at **I**, **J**, **K** and **L**.

W.S. with the gimp pairs at the centre so that each pair of gimps changes sides.

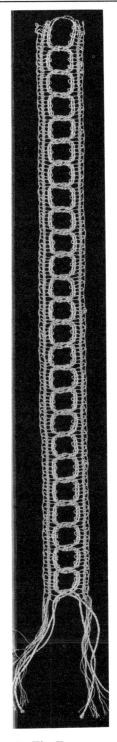

4. *The Egg*

Pattern 5:
Little Diamond

Bobbins   20 pairs

Hang 2 pairs on **A** and 2 pairs on a temporary pin inside **A**. Hang 2 pairs on **B** and 2 pairs on a temporary pin inside **B**. Hang 1 pair on each of the other 12 temporary pins.

W.S. Tw 3 with 2 right hand pairs. Give the edge pair 1 more Tw and leave. With the left hand pair, W.S. through 2 pairs. Tw 3 and put up the inside foot pin. Make $\frac{1}{2}$ St and 2 Tw with the next pair from a temporary pin. This is called the catch pin.

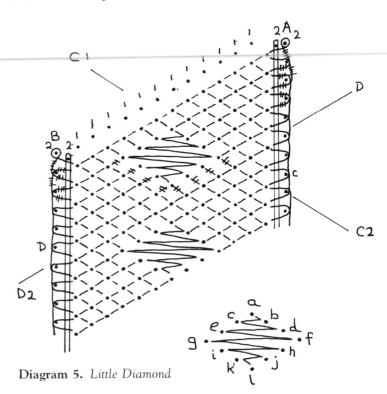

Pricking 5. *Little Diamond*

Diagram 5. *Little Diamond*

*With left hand pair make $\frac{1}{2}$ St and 2 Tw with the next pair from a temporary pin, and put up the next pin between these 2 pairs. Repeat from * with all pairs from temporary pins.

With 2 pairs on **B** W.S. Tw 3, give the edge pair 1 more Tw and leave. With right hand pair W.S. through 2 pairs, Tw 3, and put up the inside pin. $\frac{1}{2}$ St Tw 2 with the last pair from the long row. This makes another catch pin at the left. Remove the temporary pins.

On the right, continue to make footside, catch pin, and line of ground stitches, but each line shorter than the previous one until **C** is reached, and the line from **C1** to **C2** makes a triangle.

Now make the little diamond in whole stitch, bringing in pairs from right and left and making a W.S. with the first two pairs at **a**. Put up pin **a**, enclosing the pin with W.S. The right hand pair is the worker and makes W.S. through 1 pair to right. Tw 2, and put up a pin at **b**. W.S. back to left through 3 pairs, Tw 2, and put up pin **c**. Continue bringing in pairs until the diamond is at its widest point. The pairs brought in at **f** and **g** are now left out; continue leaving out one pair after **h**, **i**, **j** and **k**. At **1** there will be 2 pairs left. W.S., put up pin **1** and enclose with W.S. Tw all pairs coming from the W.S. diamond twice. Now make a section of ground and footside at the left until all pins above the line **D1** to **D2** have been worked. Make one complete row of ground between the diamonds, and also the triangle to the right of the second diamond.

The lines denoting twists on pairs of bobbins are not shown after this pattern. By now you should be familiar with the footside sequence.

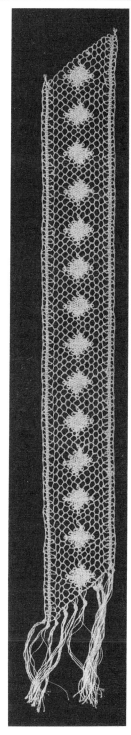

5. *Little Diamond*

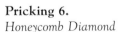

Pattern 6:

Honeycomb Diamond

Bobbins   20 pairs – Gimps   1 pair

Most Malmesbury patterns are made at an angle of 52° but a few are made at 60°, and this is one of them. If you do not want to use the straight start, use the line of pin-holes above the first gimp, crossing as temporary pin-holes, and make a diagonal line.

For the straight start
Hang 2 pairs on **A** and 2 pairs on **B**. Leave the next hole and hang 2 pairs on **C**, **D**, **E**, **F**, **G**, **H** and **I**. Hang 1 pair on each temporary pin-hole between **B** and **C** and between **G** and **H**. All pairs, except those on **B** and **H** should be hung splayed, one outside the other. Those on **B** and **H** should be hung side by side. Tw each pair twice.

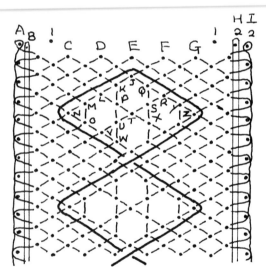

Diagram 6. *Honeycomb Diamond*

Pricking 6.
Honeycomb Diamond

With 2 pairs on **A**, W.S. Tw 3. Give the edge pair 1 extra Tw and leave. With the right hand pair, W.S. through 2 pairs and the one from the temporary pair. Tw 2 and put up the inside pin; W.S. back through 3 pairs, Tw 3, and put up the edge pin. W.S. Tw 3 with the edge pair.

*Give the edge pair 1 more Tw and leave. With the right hand pair W.S. through 2 pairs, Tw 3, and put up inside pin. With the right hand pair from the first catch pin, Tw 2. With the left hand pair from **C** Tw 2, make a ground stitch with these 2 pairs and put up the pin. With the left hand pair, $\frac{1}{2}$ St, Tw 2, with the pair hanging round the next catch pin.

Make another edge stitch and repeat from * starting with the right hand pair from **C** and left hand from **D**. Repeat again for the next line of ground, starting with right hand pair from **D** and left hand from **E**.

On the right W.S. Tw 3 with the 2 pairs on **I**. Give the edge pair one more Tw and leave. With the left hand pair W.S. through 3 pairs, Tw 3, and put up pin. W.S. back through 3 pairs and make the edge stitch. This W.S. at what is normally a catch pin may be unconventional but it gives a firm start. With the left hand pair from the first catch pin, and the right hand pair from **G**, make a ground stitch, then an edge stitch, then another catch pin, and 1 more edge stitch.

Starting the next line with the left hand pair from **G** and the right hand pair from **F**, make 3 ground stitches. Make one more row, starting with the right hand from **E** and the left hand from **F**.

Hang the gimp on a temporary pin at **J** and pass it through 5 pairs to the right and 5 pairs to the left. Tw 2 on each. Work the honeycomb diamond in alphabetical order, removing and replacing pin at **J** as you make the first honeycomb stitch − $\frac{1}{2}$ St Tw pin, $\frac{1}{2}$ St Tw.

After **Z** complete the last long line of honeycomb. Pass the gimps down through 5 pairs each side and cross at centre, right over left. Make a triangle of ground at the left and begin again at the right.

6. *Honeycomb Diamond*

Pattern 7:

Whole Stitch and Honeycomb Diamonds

Bobbins   20 pairs – Gimps   1 pair

This is the same honeycomb diamond as the previous pattern, but it was made at an angle of 52° and has alternate whole stitch diamonds. When the whole stitch diamond is complete, each pair needs 2 twists before the gimp is passed down each side.

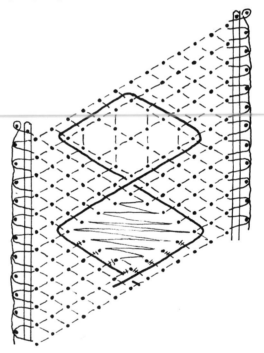

Diagram 7. *Whole Stitch and Honeycomb Diamond*

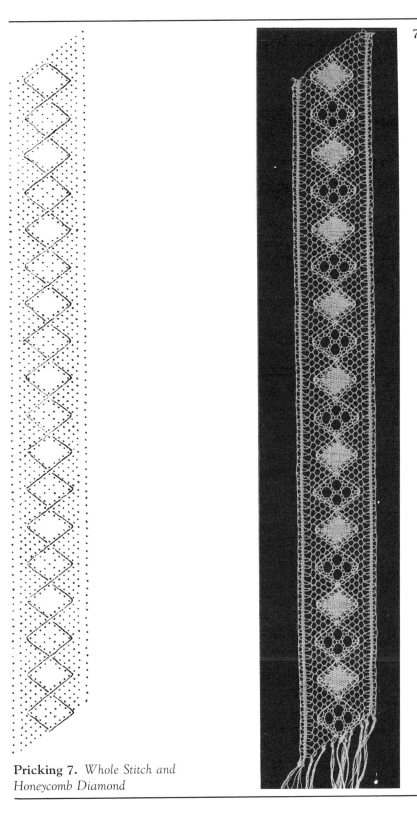

7. *Whole Stitch and Honeycomb Diamond*

Pricking 7. *Whole Stitch and Honeycomb Diamond*

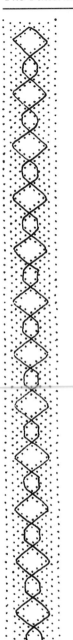

Whole Stitch Diamond and Honeycomb Ring

Bobbins   16 pairs – Gimps   1 pair

Again a straight start is used, but if you prefer a diagonal start use the pin-holes above the second crossing of the gimps as temporary pin-holes.

The whole stitch diamond is the same as the previous pattern but with only four holes on each side and one less pin-hole across the ground at each side. Therefore, at the widest point of the diamond, pass the inside pair from the catch pin inside the gimp to work W.S. at one pin-hole, then outside the gimp to work at the next catch pin.

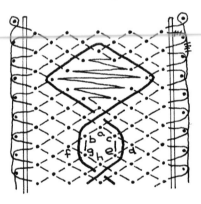

Diagram 8. *Whole Stitch Diamond and Honeycomb Ring*

Pricking 8. *Whole Stitch Diamond and Honeycomb Ring*

The honeycomb ring is worked passing 2 pairs from each side through the gimp. The centre 2 pairs make honeycomb at **a**, the 2 left hand pairs make honeycomb at **b**, the 2 right hand pairs make honeycomb at **c**. Pass the right hand pair from **c** outside the gimp to make a ground stitch at **d** and pass the left hand pair from that stitch back inside the gimp to make honeycomb at **e**.

Pass the left hand pair from **b** outside the gimp to make a ground stitch at **f** and pass the right hand pair from that stitch back inside the gimp to make a honeycomb stitch at **g**. Use the 2 centre pairs to make the last honeycomb stitch at **h**.

In some Bucks Point patterns this stitch outside the gimp is worked as a catch pin, but I have not found this in any of the Malmesbury samples.

8. *Whole Stitch Diamond and Honeycomb Ring*

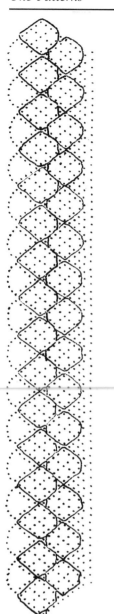

Pattern 9:

Whole Stitch Fan and Double Honeycomb Diamonds

Bobbins *20 pairs – Gimps 1 pair*

This has two honeycomb diamonds and a small fan at the headside, but note that the gimp only goes around the tip of the honeycomb diamond at the headside. At the other three diamond points the gimp passes inside the tip. Also note that one gimp is almost passive down the centre of the two diamonds while the other gimp works around the diamonds to right and left.

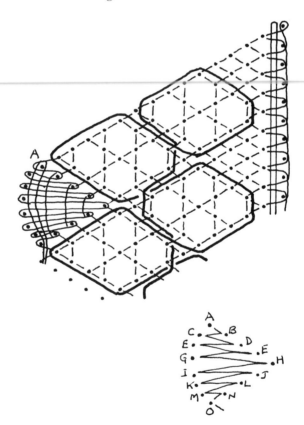

Pricking 9. *Whole Stitch Fan and Double Honeycomb Diamond*

Diagram 9. *Whole Stitch Fan and Double Honeycomb Diamond*

Work the little fan by hanging in two pairs at pin **A** and bringing the last pair from inside the honeycomb diamond above the top pin of the fan, out to the left, to become the worker for the fan, so it makes W.S. through 3 pairs to pin **B**. Work the fan in alphabetical order, in a similar manner to the W.S. diamond in Pattern 5, but pairs are only brought in on the right up to the widest point, and they are left out again one by one until three pairs remain at the bottom hole.

At each side Tw the worker pair twice before putting up the pin. After pin **O** the worker makes W.S. through 2 pairs and passes inside the gimp to work the tip of the honeycomb diamond.

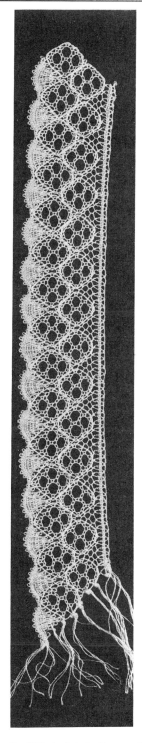

9. *Whole Stitch Fan and Double Honeycomb Diamond*

Pattern 10:

Cat's Eye

Bobbins   17 pairs – Gimps   1 pair

Work the ground triangle **A-B-C**.

Hang gimp on a temporary pin and 1 pair on each temporary pin at **D**, **E** and **F**. Pass left gimp through these 3 pairs on left, and right gimp through 3 pairs from ground.

Work honeycomb diamond. Pass gimps through 3 pairs on left and 3 pairs on right, but do not Tw pairs to enclose gimp yet. Cross gimps right over left and pass the new left one up through 3 pairs – now Tw each of these 3 to enclose both gimps.

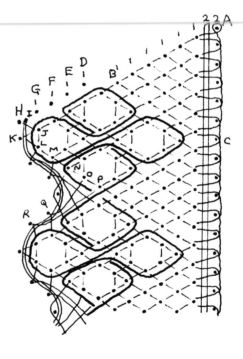

Pricking 10. *Cat's Eye*

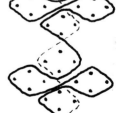

Diagram 10. *Cat's Eye*

Hang 1 pair on **G**, pass gimp through, Tw 2. Make honeycomb row with 3 pairs waiting. Hang 1 pair on **H** and 2 on **I**. With pair from **H** make W.S. through 2 to right. Pass gimp through, Tw 2. Work honeycomb pin **J**. Pass gimp through left hand pair, Tw 2. W.S. through 2.

Work picot at **K**. W.S. back to right and complete honeycomb ring. Pass gimp around the ring and diagonally up through 3 more pairs from first ring. Tw these 3 twice to enclose both gimps, pass gimp through 3 more pairs and work third honeycomb ring.

After the first ring is worked it is tempting to use the right hand gimp to work the third honeycomb ring. If this is done, the result is a gap at the centre instead of the gimp being crossed there. Work fourth honeycomb ring and cross gimps at centre.

With left hand from **L**, work out to a picot, back through 2 passives and stay there. Repeat with left hand from **M**.

With left hand from **N**, W.S. through 4 pairs, Tw 3, and put up valley pin. Make triangle of ground at right. With left hand from **O** and **P** W.S. through two pairs each.

The 2 right hand pairs from this group are now used to work the top two holes of the next honeycomb ring. Work the pair hanging to left of valley pin in W.S. through 4 pairs, and this works the left pin of the same ring.

The third pair from the left makes W.S. through 2 pairs, picot at **Q**, W.S. back through 3 pairs, to make the top pin of the next ring. Again, the third pair from the left makes W.S. through 2 pairs to make picot **R**, and W.S. back through 2 pairs to continue the ring.

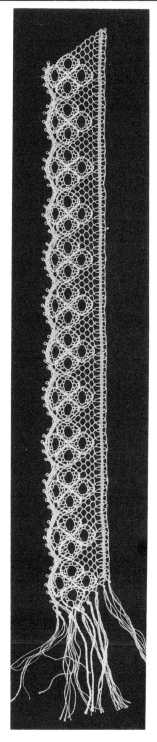

10. *Cat's Eye*

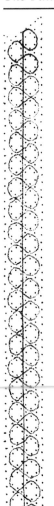

Pricking 11. *Double Chain*

Pattern 11:
Double Chain

Bobbins   13 pairs – Gimps   1 pair

This is worked entirely in honeycomb stitch except for the foot pin on each side. A pair of gimps is used, but one is really a 'passive' passing straight down the centre of the pattern.

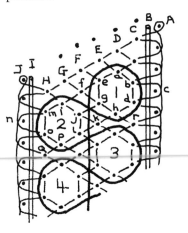

Diagram 11. *Double Chain*

Hang 2 pairs on **A**, splayed. Hang 2 pairs on **B** side by side. Hang one pair each above **C** to **G**. Nothing on **H**. Hang 2 pairs on **I** side by side and 2 pairs on **J** splayed.

Work 1 complete row across the pattern. This will not be repeated. Work another foot pin on the left and on the right a foot pin, one honeycomb stitch, and another foot pin. Introduce the gimp on a temporary pin at **a**. Pass 2 pairs from the left inside the gimp and 2 pairs from the right. The last pair on the right will be the footside worker pair. Tw these 4 pairs twice and begin the honeycomb ring with the centre 2 pairs replacing pin **a**. After pin **b** pass the right hand pair outside the gimp, Tw twice, W.S. through 2 pairs, to make the foot pin at **c**, and W.S. back through 2 pairs. Tw twice and pass it back inside the gimp to continue honeycomb at **d**. After **e** pass the left hand pair outside the gimp to make honeycomb at **f**, and pass the right hand back inside the gimp to make honeycomb at **g** and finish the honeycomb at **h**.

Bring the right hand gimp around and cross the gimps with the left hand from **g** enclosing both gimps. Pass the new left hand gimp through 3 more pairs. The last pair will be the footside worker from the left. Begin the second honeycomb ring with the centre 2 pairs. Honeycomb at **i**. After **j** the right hand pair passes the passive gimp to work honeycomb at **k**, and the left from **k** goes back inside the gimp to work **l**. After **m** the left hand pair passes outside the gimp to make the footside pin at **n**, and back through the gimp to make honeycomb at **o**. Complete the honeycomb ring at **p**. Make another foot pin at the right and honeycomb at **r**.

Pass the left hand gimp up, cross right over left with the right hand pair from **l**, enclosing both gimps, and continue to pass the new right hand gimp up through 3 more pairs. The last one is the footside pair from the right.

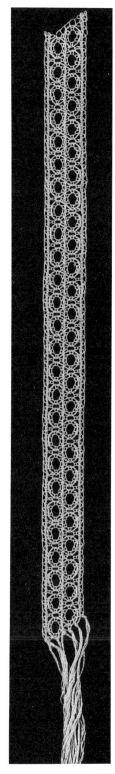

11. *Double Chain*

Pattern 12:
Chain and
Whole Stitch Chevron

Bobbins   17 pairs – Gimps   1 pair

Set up and work triangle **A-B-C**.

Introduce the gimp on a temporary pin at **D**. Hang 1 pair on **E** and 1 pair on **F** and pass the gimp through them. Also pass the pairs from 1st and 2nd rows of ground inside gimp. Tw 2 on each. With centre 2 pairs make honeycomb stitch, replacing pin **D**. Make honeycomb stitch at **G**, pass the right hand pair outside the gimp to

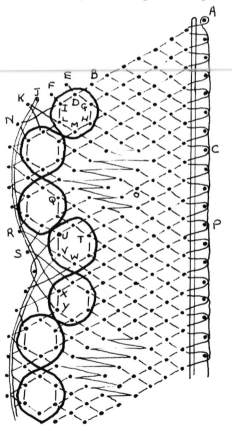

Diagram 12. *Chain and Whole Stitch Chevron*

make a ground stitch, and pass the left hand pair back inside the gimp to make honeycomb at **H**. Make honeycomb at **I** and pass left hand pair outside the gimp.

Hang 2 pairs on **J** side by side and 2 pairs on **K** splayed. Make a false picot with the 2 pairs on **K**. With the right hand pair, W.S. through 3 pairs, pass inside the gimp and work honeycomb at **L**. Complete the honeycomb ring at **M**. Pass the gimps to centre and cross right over left. Pass the new left hand gimp up through 2 pairs, Tw 2 on each.

With the left hand pair from the false picot at **K**, W.S. through 3 pairs, and pass inside gimp to begin the next honeycomb ring. Third from edge make picot at **N**. W.S. back through 2 pairs to pass inside gimp. This pair will continue to pass in and out along the headside. It makes a honeycomb stitch between the second and third rings outside the gimp.

At the right of the second honeycomb ring a line of ground stitch has to be completed before that ring can be finished.

A line of ground above the chevron is worked down to the footside, then the top half of the chevron is worked in W.S., bringing in pairs from right and left, and leaving 1 pair out on the right after the third, fifth and seventh rows. A small triangle of footside and ground is worked from **C-OP** and the bottom of the chevron can be completed. Note that this is an irregular chevron, the bottom half being narrower and shorter than the top half. The pairs coming out of the chevron need 2 Tws.

Cross the gimps between the two headside rings and pass the gimps through 2 pairs each side. Begin the third honeycomb ring with the centre 2 pairs. After **Q** the right hand pair passes outside the gimp to begin a ground row – work 3 pin-holes in ground stitch. The left hand pair passes back inside the gimp to continue the honeycomb ring. After picot **R**, the picot pair returns through 2 pairs in W.S. The left hand pair from the bottom of the honeycomb ring makes W.S. through 3 pairs; picot **S**, and return to third place.

Cross the gimps and pass the new right hand gimp up through 2 pairs, and also through 2 pairs from the ground. Tw 2 on each and begin the fourth ring with the centre 2 pairs. After **T** the right hand pair passes outside the gimp

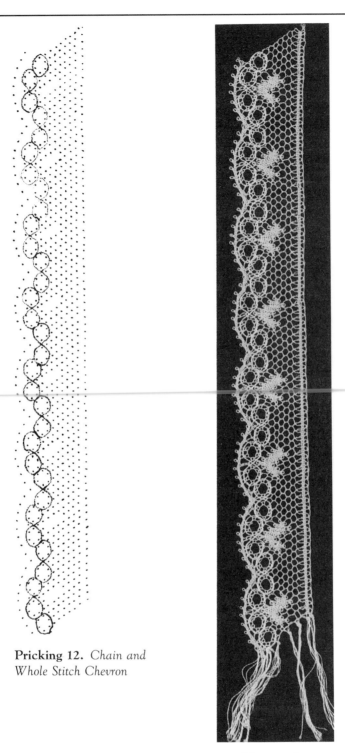

Pricking 12. *Chain and Whole Stitch Chevron*

12. *Chain and Whole Stitch Chevron*

to work a ground stitch, and the left hand pair passes back inside the gimp to continue the honeycomb ring.

The left hand pair from **U** passes outside the gimp. W.S. through 4 pairs, Tw 3 and put up the valley pin. Tw the pair to the left of the gimp twice and pass it inside the gimp to work honeycomb at **V**. This pair now passes outside the gimp and makes W.S. through 2 pairs to become a passive headside pair. The picot pair from **S**, (fourth from edge) makes W.S. through 1 pair and passes inside the gimp to begin the next honeycomb ring. Use the inside pair of the original headside passives at **X** and with the valley pair W.S. through 4 pairs to work **Y**.

Pattern 13:

'Annie's Pattern' Malmesbury Fan and Honeycomb Ground

Bobbins   15 pairs – no gimp

Set up and work the triangle of honeycomb ground **A-B-C**. (See Pattern 15 for note on honeycomb ground.) Work in numerical order.

Hang 3 pairs on small letter **a** side by side at the top of the fan.

Pricking 13. *Annie's Pattern*

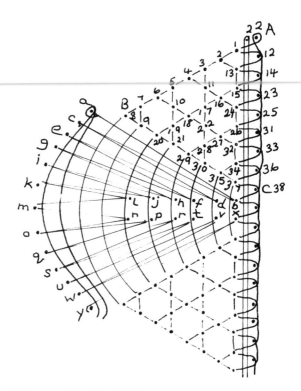

Diagram 13. *Annie's Pattern*

Work the fan in alphabetical order, starting with the left hand pair, which makes W.S. through the other two pairs on **a** and continues in W.S. through all the other pairs, from the honeycomb ground to **b**. W.S. Tw 2 with the footside worker at **b** and make up another footside pin below **C**. Bring the worker back through 2 pairs in W.S., ready to work the same W.S. Tw 2 at pin **x**.

With the left hand from **b**, continue to make the fan. Leave out one pair each at **b**, **d**, **f**, **h**, **j**, **l**, and after each has been twisted twice bring them in at **n**, **p**, **r**, **t**, **v** and **x**. When the fan is complete, put up pin **y** with the worker to the left of it, and the two passive pairs which are not used in the honeycomb triangle remain inside the pin.

13. *Annie's Pattern*

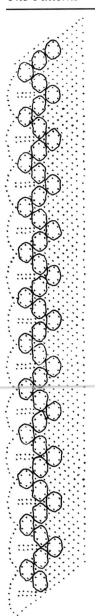

Pattern 14:
Fan and Chain

Bobbins   20 pairs – Gimps   1 pair

Set up and work the small triangle **A-B-C**. Hang gimp on a temporary pin at **D**. Hang 1 pair on each support pin **E-F**.

Pass 2 pairs from left and 2 pairs from right inside the gimp and work the first honeycomb ring, starting with the two centre pairs and replacing pin **D**. When the ring is complete, the gimps are crossed at the left, and the new left hand gimp is passed up through 2 pairs, and through 2 new pairs from the support pins above.

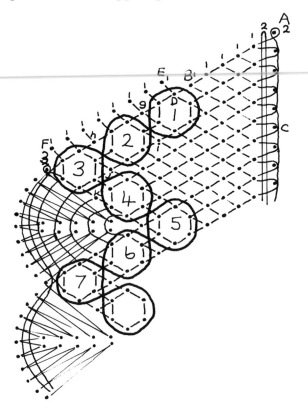

Pricking 14. *Fan and Chain*

Diagram 14. *Fan and Chain*

Pin **g** is worked as a ground stitch in my sample, also **h**, **i**, **j** and **k** and so on. But I have seen another sample of this pattern where all those pin-holes were worked in honeycomb stitch, as in Pattern 11.

Honeycomb rings 2 and 3 are made, then 6 rows of ground stitch, and then rings 4 and 5. These are followed by the little fan, which is the same as in 'Annie's Pattern' (Pattern 13) except at the valley where one pair of passives from the fan makes a W.S. outside the gimp, with the pair coming from the top left hole of ring 7.

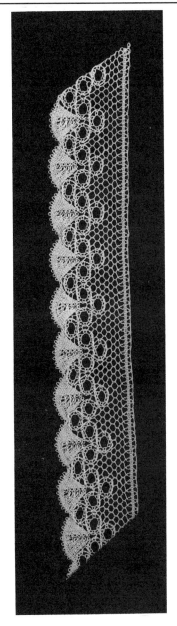

14. *Fan and Chain*

Pattern 15:

Honeycomb and One Gimp

Bobbins *13 pairs – Gimps* *1 single*

Hang 2 pairs splayed on **A**, W.S. Tw 3 left hand, Tw 4 right hand. Hang 2 pairs side by side on temporary pin. With left hand pair from **A**, W.S. through these two pairs to left, Tw 2. (**Note** in Honeycomb this pair only has 2 Tws.) Hang 1 pair on temporary pins above **2**, **3** and **4**. Honeycomb stitch at each of these pin-holes. Hang 2 pairs at **6** and 2 passive pairs on a temporary pin inside them. Hang the single gimp inside these 4 pairs.

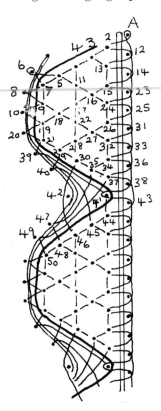

Pricking 15. *Honeycomb and One Gimp*

Diagram 15. *Honeycomb and One Gimp*

Make a false picot at **6** and with right hand pair W.S. through the 2 passive pairs, pass the gimp through this pair and make honeycomb at **5**. Pass the left hand pair from **6** through 2 passives and gimp to make honeycomb at **7**. Remove temporary pins. Leave gimp pin.

Use the left hand pair to make picot at **8**. Bring it back in to work **9** and out again to work **10**. Leave. With pairs from **4** and **5**, honeycomb at **11**. Leave both pairs.

Footside at **12**. With left hand pair W.S. through 2, Tw 2, and honeycomb at **13** with pair from **3**.

Footside at **14**. W.S. through 2 pairs, honeycomb at **15, 16, 17, 18** and **19**. Picot at **20**. Following the numbers, complete the honeycomb to **38**. Picot at **39**. Pass gimp down through 5 pairs including foot workers. Follow it with pair from picot at **39** and use this pair to make W.S., Tw 2, at **41** with foot worker. This holds the gimp firmly in place. From **41** the right hand pair passes the gimp and goes out to **43**.

The left hand pair drops straight down – pass the gimp through it, to begin the long line of honeycomb at **44**. The pair from picot **40** will W.S. back through 2 pairs to become the third passive, and will work honeycomb at **45**. The pair from **30** will W.S. out through 4 pairs, Tw 2, and put up the valley pin. W.S. back through 4 pairs to make honeycomb at **46**.

The pair from **35**, third from edge, will make the next picot at **47**, and W.S. through 3 pairs to make honeycomb at **48**.

The pair from **37**, third from edge, will make the next picot at **49**, and W.S. through 2 pairs to make honeycomb at **50**.

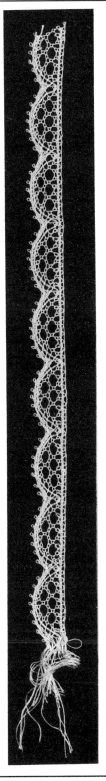

15. *Honeycomb and One Gimp*

Pattern 16:

Honeycomb Fan and Four Pin Bud

Bobbins   20 pairs – Gimps   1 single and 1 pair

Set up and work the triangle **A-B-C**. Hang 1 pair each on temporary pins at **D** and **E**. Introduce the gimp pair on **F** and pass 2 pairs from each side through it. Tw 2 on each.

Make honeycomb stitch with the 2 centre pairs replacing pin **F**. Honeycomb at **g** with the 2 right hand pairs. Honeycomb at **h** with the 2 left hand pairs. Remove temporary pins **D** and **E**. Honeycomb at **i** with the 2 centre pairs.

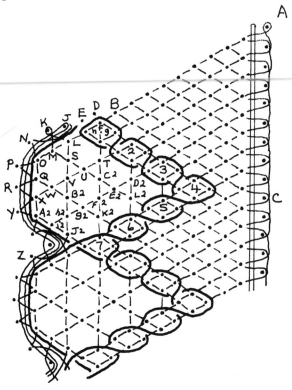

Diagram 16. *Honeycomb Fan and Four Pin Bud*

Pass the gimps around and cross them between **g** and **i**. Pass the new right hand gimp through 3 pairs, and the left hand gimp through 1 pair, and begin the second bud with the 2 centre pairs.

Make up buds 3 and 4 and begin the headside. Hang a single gimp from a temporary pin at **E** and 3 pairs on a pin at **J**, side by side. Hang another 2 pairs on a pin at **K**, splayed. Tw 3 and make a false picot. The right hand pair makes W.S. through 3 pairs from **J**, Tw 2, pass the single gimp through it, Tw 2 and honeycomb at **L**.

The left hand pair from **K** also makes W.S. through 3 pairs, and passes inside the gimp to make honeycomb at **M**.

The third pair from the edge makes W.S. out through 2 pairs and an ordinary picot at **N**, then W.S. back through 2 pairs. Pass it inside the gimp and work honeycomb at **O**. This pair continues to work in and out at the headside.

Continue to make the honeycomb fan in alphabetical order; after **Y**, continue with **A2**, etc.

After the last picot, that pair returns to third place from the edge and will begin the honeycomb in the next fan. The next pair from the honeycomb fan makes W.S. through 3 pairs. Tw 3 and put up the valley pin and leave the headside. Make up honeycomb buds 5, 6 and 7, followed by a triangle of footside and ground.

To the left of bud 7, the headside gimp crosses with the left hand gimp of the pair.

The left pair (JZ) from the honeycomb in the first fan makes W.S. through 4 pairs to make picot **Z**, and W.S. back through the 2 passive pairs.

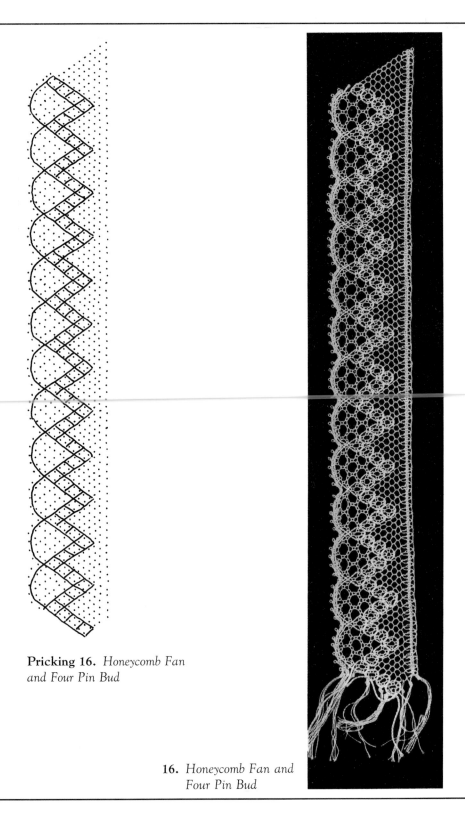

Pricking 16. *Honeycomb Fan and Four Pin Bud*

16. *Honeycomb Fan and Four Pin Bud*

Pattern 17:

Clover Leaf

Bobbins   24 pairs – Gimps   1 pair

Set up and work first row right across pattern. Work second row to the top of leaf **b**. Work triangle **A** with a tally on the third row.

Introduce the gimp at the centre. Pass it through 3 pairs on each side. Normally the gimp thread is enclosed by 2 twists before and after it is passed through a pair, but in this case do not twist after the gimp is passed through.

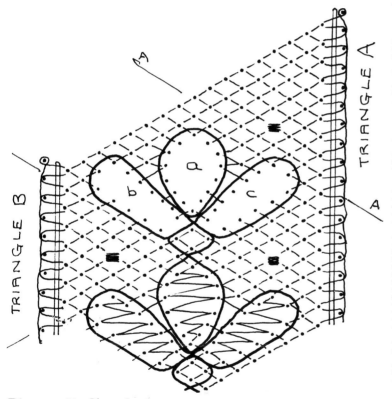

Diagram 17. *Clover Leaf*

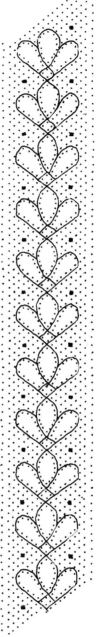

Pricking 17. *Clover Leaf*

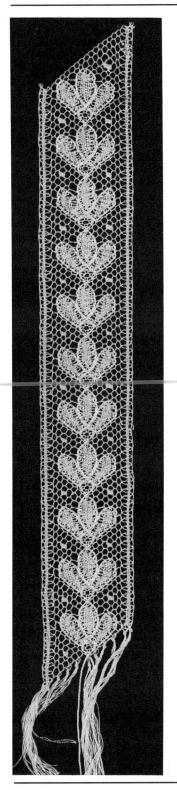

Begin leaf **a** with the 2 centre pairs. Work a W.S., Tw the weaver twice. In this case the weaver is the right hand pair. Continue working W.S., bringing in 1 pair each side. After the fourth row let the right and left pairs pass outside the gimp, giving them 2 Tws after passing out. Each pair makes a ground stitch and passes back inside the gimp. Work rows 5 and 6 and leave out 1 pair on each side.

Work rows 7 and 8 without leaving out a pair.

Work rows 9 and 10 and leave out a pair each side.

Work rows 11 and 12 without leaving out a pair.

Finish at the bottom pin with leaving 1 pair at each side. Pass the gimps down each side, cross at the centre, right over left, and pass the new left hand pair up through 7 pairs.

Begin leaf **b** with centre top pairs (second and third from left inside the gimp), make a W.S., and Tw twice on the left pair. Pin up. Continue in whole stitch bringing in pairs as on the diagram. After row 2 the left hand pair passes the gimp, 2 twists and ground stitch. The right hand pair passes back inside the gimp. After the third row bring in pairs on alternate holes on the right, but leave out 1 pair at each hole on the left. After enclosing the bottom pin, 1 pair passes out to the ground on the left and the other passes to the four pin bud on the right of it.

Pass the gimp down the left side of leaf **b**, then up, and cross gimps right over left at the centre. Pass the new right hand gimp up through 7 pairs and start leaf **c**.

Make a W.S. with the second and third pairs from the right inside the gimp. Twist the right hand pair twice and put up the pin. Continue in W.S. After the second row the right hand pair passes out to make a ground stitch and back inside the gimp. Bring in a pair from the left on alternate rows and leave out 1 pair after every row on the right. Finish at the bottom pin with 1 pair passing out to the ground on the right and one pair passing to the centre bud. Pass the gimp down the right side of leaf **c** and up through 2 pairs. Cross gimps and pass the new left hand one down through 2 pairs. Tw twice on each of the 4 pairs

17. *Clover Leaf*

inside the gimp. Make a honeycomb stitch with the 2 centre pairs. Then, honeycomb with the 2 right hand pairs and the 2 left hand pairs, and then with the 2 centre pairs again. Pass the gimps through 2 pairs each and cross them at the centre.

Triangle **B** can now be worked, making a tally on the third row. Rows 4 to 7 are shorter, but must be worked to have the necessary pairs to pass inside the gimp to work the next leaf **b**.

Triangle **A** can now be started again, but there is no continuous line right across the work as at the start.

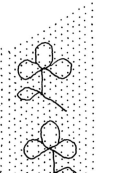

Pattern 18:
Little Flower

Bobbins 21 pairs – Gimps 1 pair with 1 full bobbin and a small amount on the second

Set up across pattern and work the triangle on the right.

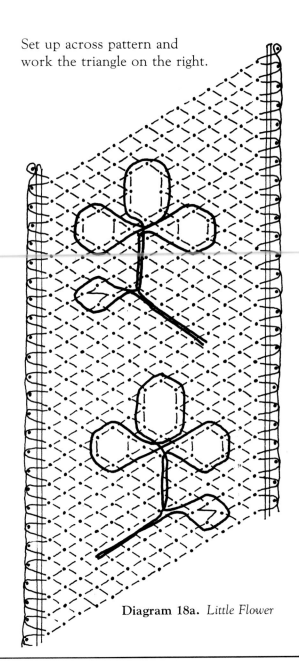

Pricking 18. *Little Flower*

Diagram 18a. *Little Flower*

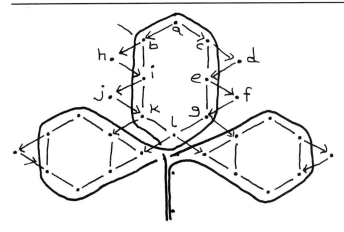

Diagram 18b. *Little Flower*

Introduce the gimp at the centre and pass two pairs from right and two pairs from left inside the gimp. Tw twice on each and begin the honeycomb centre. This has three pinholes down each side, so the right hand pair from **c** will pass outside the gimp to make a ground stitch at **d**, and the left hand from **d** will pass back inside the gimp to work honeycomb at **e**. The right hand from **e** will pass outside the gimp to work a ground stitch at **f**, and the left hand from **f** will pass back inside the gimp to work honeycomb at **g**. The left hand from **b** will pass outside the gimp to work a ground stitch at **h**, and the right hand from **h** will pass back inside the gimp to work honeycomb at **i**. The left hand from **i** will pass outside the gimp to make a ground stitch at **j**, and the right hand from **j** will pass inside the gimp to work honeycomb at **k**. The right hand from **k** and the left hand from **g** will make honeycomb at **l**.

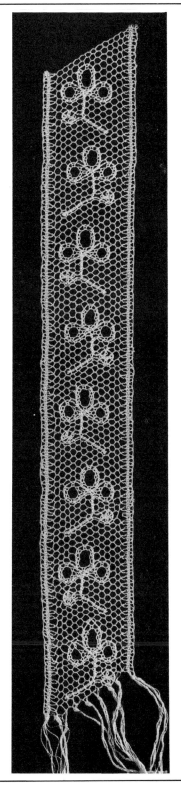

18. *Little Flower*

Pattern 19:
Hexagon and Honeycomb Rings

Bobbins   24 pairs – Gimps   1 pair

Set up and work a line of ground stitch right across the pattern. Work the triangle **A-B-C**. Introduce the gimp at the centre and pass it down each side through 6 pairs.

Pricking 19. *Hexagon and Honeycomb Ring*

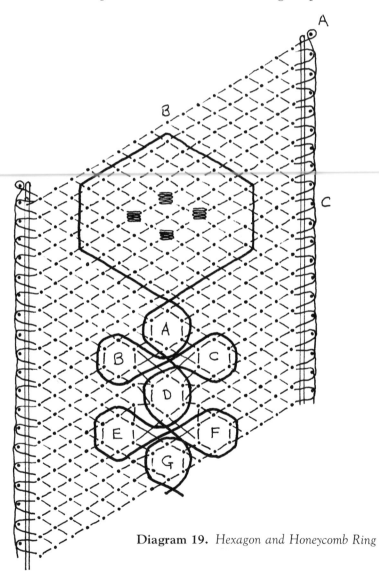

Diagram 19. *Hexagon and Honeycomb Ring*

To keep the gimps vertical at each side pass a pair outside the gimp to make a ground stitch, and pass a pair from this stitch back inside to make another ground stitch there.

See Pattern 24 for instructions on working the honeycomb rings. The pin-holes in ring **D** are out of line with those surrounding it, but this follows the original Malmesbury pricking.

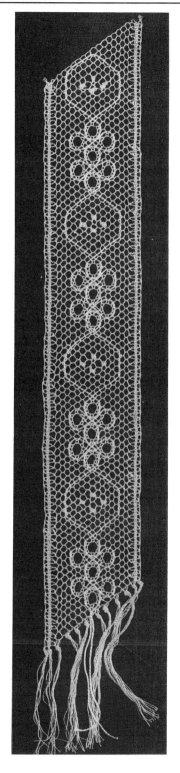

19. *Hexagon and Honeycomb Ring*

Pattern 20:
Bat and Ball

Bobbins   20 pairs – Gimps   1 pair

Work triangle **A**-**B**-**C**. At the bottom of the triangle only the holes above the gimp line can be worked, but be sure to work to **C**. Hang the gimp on **D** and pass the right hand gimp through all except the last 4 pairs.

Begin to make the honeycomb ring near the footside with the second and third pairs inside the gimp making honeycomb at **1**. Make honeycomb at **2** and **3**, pass the right hand pair from **3** outside the gimp, to make a catch pin stitch at **4** with the footside worker, and pass it back inside the gimp to make honeycomb at **5**.

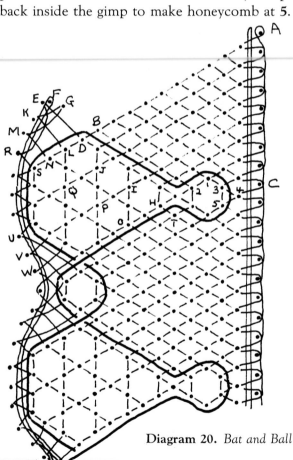

Diagram 20. *Bat and Ball*

Pricking 20. *Bat and Ball*

Leave these and go back to the headside. Hang 2 pairs on **E**, splayed, and 2 pairs on **F**, side by side. Hang 2 more pairs on **G**, splayed.

With the pairs on **E** Tw 3, make a false picot and with the right hand pair, W.S. through 4 pairs. Pass the left hand gimp through this pair and make a honeycomb stitch, replacing pin **D**. Continue a long line of honeycomb which will complete the honeycomb ring near the footside.

On the way back to the headside make up honeycomb stitches in the 'gap' row at **H**, **I** and **J**. The left hand pair from **E** makes W.S. through 2 pairs to third place from the edge. The left hand pair from **G** makes W.S. through 3 pairs, and an ordinary picot at **K**, then W.S. through 4 pairs. Pass it inside the gimp to make honeycomb at **L**.

The right hand pair from **G**, now fourth from the edge, makes W.S. through 3 pairs and picot at **M**. W.S. through 3 pairs, and pass inside the gimp to begin a long line of honeycomb at **N**. When that line is complete, make up the 'gap' row on the way back to the headside at **O**, **P** and **Q**.

The third pair from the edge makes W.S. through 2 pairs to make picot **R**, and W.S. back through 2 pairs. Pass it inside the gimp to make honeycomb at **S**. This pair will pass in and out along the headside.

Complete the honeycomb inside the gimp line and pass each gimp down to cross at the centre. Three lines of ground are worked: the pin at **T** holds the gimp up in place, and the first line of ground is made starting with the pairs each side of this pin.

After picot **U**, the picot pair makes W.S. through 5 pairs, and then passes inside the new left hand gimp to work the top pin-hole of the honeycomb ring.

After picot **V**, the picot pair makes W.S. through 4 pairs and passes inside the gimp to make the top left pin-hole of the honeycomb ring. The left hand pair from this pin-hole passes outside the gimp.

The picot pair from **W** makes W.S. through 4 pairs and passes inside the gimp to make the bottom left

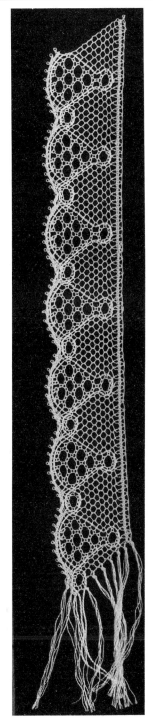

20. *Bat and Ball*

honeycomb. The left hand pair from the last pin-hole above the crossed gimps will now be third from the edge, and with it make W.S. through 2 pairs, Tw 3, and put up the valley pin. When the honeycomb ring is complete and the gimps are crossed again, this valley pair will make whole stitch through 5 pairs and pass inside the gimp to begin the next honeycomb section.

There is another version of 'Bat and Ball' with more honeycomb rings, but this is the one which best represents its name.

Pattern 21:
Honeycomb Ring and Diamond with 'Fingers'

Bobbins *20 pairs – Gimps* ***1 pair. Wind only a small amount of gimp on 1 of the pair***

This is another pattern made at 60° and with a straight start. If you prefer a diagonal start, just use one of the complete diagonal lines before the second motif.

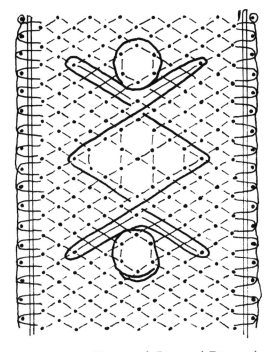

Diagram 21. *Honeycomb Ring and Diamond with Fingers*

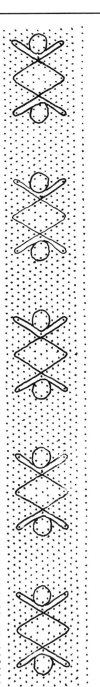

Pricking 21. *Honeycomb Ring and Diamond with Fingers*

Work the honeycomb ring, bring the gimps around and cross them, then pass each gimp up through 5 pairs. Tw 2 on each pair. Make honeycomb stitch with the last 2 pairs the gimp passed through. On the left, the right hand pair from this stitch makes W.S. through 3 pairs, and on the

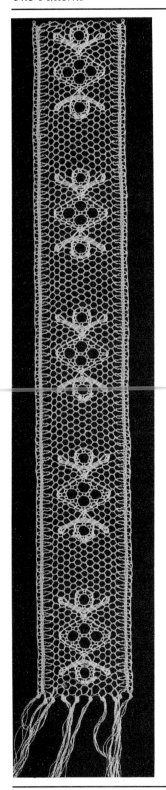

right the left hand pair from this stitch makes W.S. through 3 pairs. Tw 2 on each. Make honeycomb stitch with the 2 centre pairs and bring each gimp down to cross at the centre.

Make a triangle of ground at each side, and pass 5 pairs each side inside the gimp to work a honeycomb diamond.

When the diamond is complete bring the gimps down and cross them. Make another triangle of group at each side. Five pairs from each side are brought past the gimp. Tw 2 on each. Make honeycomb stitch with the centre 2 pairs, and each pair makes W.S. through 3 pairs and another honeycomb stitch. Tw 2 on each, pass the gimps up through 5 pairs, and cross them at the centre.

Pass each new gimp through 2 pairs and begin the last honeycomb ring. At the bottom of the ring cross the gimps, pass them up through 2 pairs each side and lay them back. When cut off, discard the small amount of thread left on one bobbin and wind another length off the full bobbin on to the empty one.

21. *Honeycomb Ring and Diamond with Fingers*

Pattern 22:
Triple Honeycomb Diamond with 'Fingers'

Bobbins *22 pairs – Gimps* *1 pair*

Set up complete row across the pattern. Make the triangle of ground **a-b-c**. Introduce gimp and pass the 2 centre pairs through. Tw 2 on each, and make a honeycomb stitch inside gimp. Pass both pairs out again to right and left. Tw 2 on each and make 2 ground stitches each side.

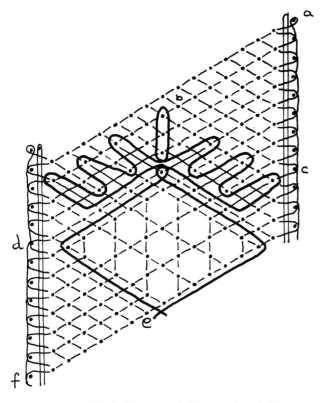

Diagram 22. *Triple Honeycomb Diamond with Fingers*

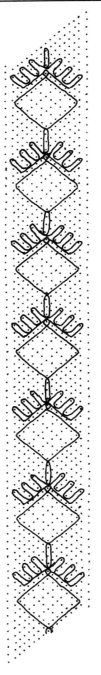

Pricking 22. *Triple Honeycomb Diamond with Fingers*

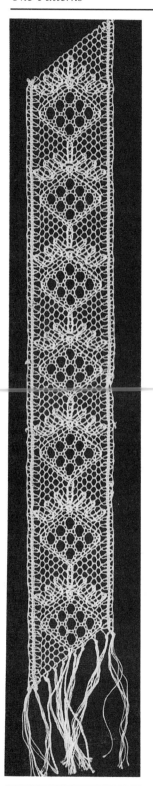

Pass the 2 centre pairs back through the gimp. Tw 2 on each and make another honeycomb stitch. Pass both pairs out again to right and left. Tw 2 on each and make 1 ground stitch each side.

Pass the centre 2 pairs back in again and Tw 2 on each. Make another honeycomb stitch and pass both pairs out to right and left again. Cross gimps right over left.

Pass left gimp up through 4 pairs, Tw 2 on each pair. Honeycomb stitch with 2 left hand pairs. With the right of these, W.S. through remaining 2 pairs. Tw 2 on each pair and leave right hand pair. Pass gimp down through 3 pairs. Tw 2 on each pair.

Starting with next left hand pair outside gimp, make 3 ground stitches. Pass gimp up through 5 pairs. Leave right hand pair. Tw 2 on other 4 pairs.

Honeycomb stitch with 2 left hand pairs. With the right hand of these, W.S. through remaining 2 pairs. Tw 2 on each pair and leave right hand pair. Pass gimp down through 3 pairs. Tw 2 on each pair.

Start with next left hand pair and make 3 ground stitches. Make footside and bring worker back. Pass gimp through 5 pairs. Leave right hand pair. Tw 2 on the other 4 pairs. The left hand of these is the worker from the footside.

Instead of the usual catch pin, a honeycomb stitch is worked inside the gimp. The right hand pair makes W.S. through 2 pairs. Tw 2 and leave. Tw 2 on other 2 pairs and pass gimp down through 3 pairs.

The left hand of these can now make the footside, catch pin and 1 ground stitch. Then the footside and catch pin, and finally the footside and the worker, comes back in W.S. through the 2 passive pairs. Tw 3 times and leave to await the next row.

Now pass the gimp up through 5 pairs, towards the centre. Only those pairs coming from a W.S. row should be twisted. Where the gimps pass each other they should have no Tws between. Tw 2 each pair after the gimp.

22. *Triple Honeycomb Diamond with Fingers*

Now work the 'gimp fingers' to the right. Pass right hand gimp up through 4 pairs. Tw 2 on each pair. Honeycomb stitch with 2 right hand pairs. With left of these, work W.S. through remaining 2 pairs. Tw 2 on each pair and leave left hand pair.

Pass gimp down through 3 pairs. Tw 2 on each. Starting with right hand pair outside the gimp, make 3 ground stitches. Pass gimp up through 5 pairs. Leave left hand pair. Tw 2 on other 4 pairs. Honeycomb stitch with 2 right hand pairs. With left of these, W.S. through remaining 2 pairs. Tw 2 on each and leave left hand pair.

Pass gimp down through 3 pairs. Tw 2 on each. Starting with right hand pair outside the gimp, make 3 ground stitches. Pass gimp up through 5 pairs. Leave left hand pair. Tw 2 on other 4 pairs. Right hand of these is the worker from the footside and again, instead of the usual catch pin, work a honeycomb stitch, and with the left hand pair make W.S. through the remaining 2 pairs. Tw 2 and leave.

Tw 2 on the other 3 pairs and pass the gimp down through 3 pairs. Tw 2 on each. Right hand of these can now make footside, catch pin and 1 ground stitch, then footside and catch pin, and finally footside and the worker, comes back through 2 passives. Tw 3 times and leave to await the next row.

Pass the gimp up through 5 pairs. All except the top pair are twisted twice. Then cross the gimp and pass through the 2 centre pairs. Tw 2 on each and make honeycomb stitch. Pass gimps through 1 pair each and cross them again. Tw 2 on each pair and make a ground row on each side, including the footside.

Make sure the gimp is crossed at centre and pass each gimp down through 7 pairs. Tw 2 on each. Make honeycomb diamond. When the diamond is finished, pass the gimps down each side. Tw 2 on each pair. Cross gimps at centre.

Make triangle of ground on the left (**d-e-f**) and return to right to start another triangle **a-b-c**.

Pattern 23:

Triple Honeycomb and Basket Filling

Bobbins   34 pairs – Gimps   3 pairs

This would make a good bookmark or fingerplate.
For instructions on beginning see Pattern 24. Three pairs of
gimps are required, one of which needs a very small
amount of thread, as it is only used across the top of
the pattern and is then laid back.

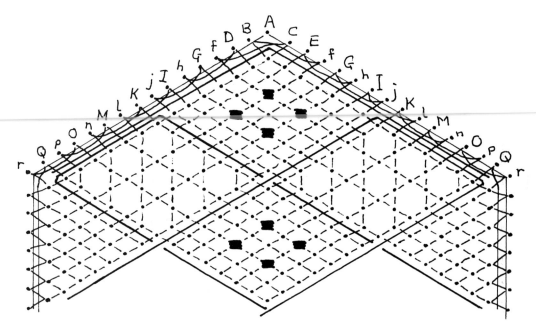

Diagram 23. *Triple Honeycomb and Basket Filling*

False picots are made at capital letters only. Ordinary
picots are made at small letters, **f, h, j, l, n, p,** and **r** on
each side.

The second and third pairs of gimps are hung above the
pin-holes, which start honeycomb adjacent to **K**.

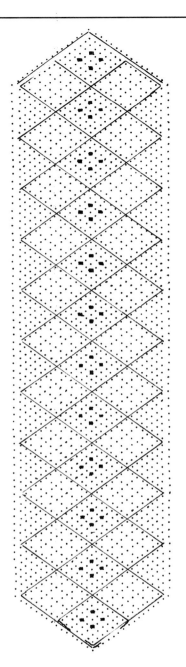

Pricking 23. *Triple Honeycomb and Basket Filling*

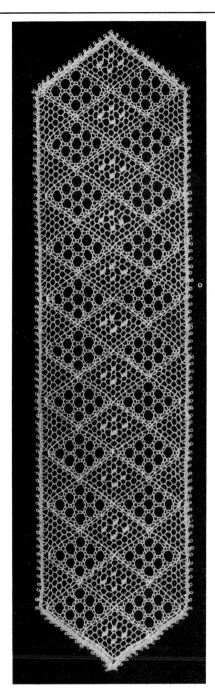

23. *Triple Honeycomb and Basket Filling*

Pattern 24:

Hexagon Motif

Bobbins   28 pairs – Gimps   2 pairs

Make false picots at **A, B, C, D** and **E.** With left pair
from **A** W.S. through 4 pairs to left. With right pair
from **A** W.S. through 4 pairs to right. These two pairs
will remain constant passives. W.S. with the 2 centre pairs.

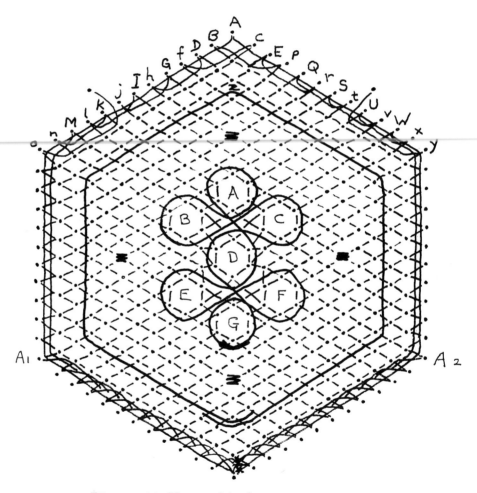

Diagram 24. *Hexagon Motif*

With left pair from **B** W.S. through 1 pair to right, twist twice and leave. With right pair from **C** W.S. through 1 pair to left. Twist twice and make a ground stitch at centre with left pair.

With right pair from **D** W.S. through 1 pair to right, twist twice, and ground stitch with left hand pair from previous stitch.

With third pair from left, W.S. through 2 pairs to left, make an ordinary picot at **f**, and W.S. back through 2 pairs. Tw twice and make a ground stitch.

Add 2 more pairs at **G** with a false picot. With right hand pair W.S. through 2 pairs to right, Tw twice, make a ground stitch. Left hand pair from **G** makes W.S. through 1 pair.

Third from left W.S. through 2 pairs. Make an ordinary picot at **h**. W.S. through 2 pairs, twist 2, make ground stitch.

Continue to add pairs with false picot at capital letters **I**, **K**, **M**. Before **K**, hang 1 extra pair on a temporary pin. Pass it over 2 passives and bring it in as the third pair from the edge. This pair will be used to work pin **O**. When the

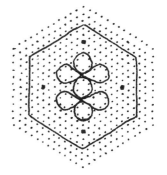

Pricking 24. *Hexagon Motif*

24. *Hexagon Motif*

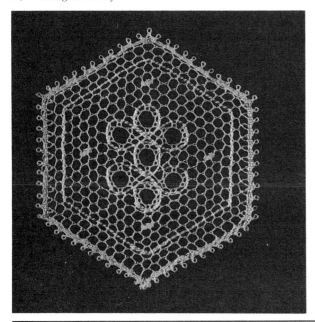

picot has been made at **O**, begin to make a footside on the left, with catch pin and stitch inside the 2 passives.

Go back to the right hand side. With left hand pair from **E** make W.S. through 1 pair, Tw 2, and make ground stitch. With third from right W.S. through 2 pairs, Tw 3, make picot at **p**. W.S. back through 2 pairs. Make ground stitch.

Add pairs with false picot at **Q**. With left hand pair W.S. through 2 pairs, Tw 2, make ground stitch. With right hand pair W.S. through 1 pair. With third pair from right W.S. through 2 pairs, Tw 3, make picot at **r**, W.S. through 2 pairs, and make ground stitch.

Add 2 pairs with false picot at **S**. With left hand pair W.S. through 2 pairs, make a ground stitch. With right hand pair, W.S. through 1 and leave. Beginning at centre, make 1 more ground row to *left*, ending with a catch pin – make edge stitch.

Make 4 ground stitches on right and introduce gimp at **Z** passing it through 10 pairs on left, and 4 pairs on right.

Make 2 ground rows to left and a tally in the third row. Make fourth row. Continue on right making ordinary picot at **t**, adding 1 pair on temporary pin and bringing it over 2 passives to lie third from edge.

Add 2 more pairs at **U** and bring them into the work. Make an ordinary picot at **v** and add the last 2 pairs at **W**. Make another ordinary picot at **x**, and the extra pair added before **u**, which has been a third passive, makes the last picot at **y**, with the next pin inside worked as a catch pin. Work 1 more ground row on right. Pass gimp down the line and work section of ground inside gimp. Introduce a second pair of gimps and begin working centre motif.

Pass gimp through 2 pairs to right and left, honeycomb at centre, right and left.

Pass left and right pairs outside gimp, Tw 2 and make ground stitch. Pass 1 pair each side back through gimp. Complete 3 bottom holes in honeycomb. Pass gimps down and cross right over left at centre. Pass new left hand gimp up through 5 pairs. Where gimps lie together there are no twists between.

Make top centre honeycomb and left honeycomb, and pass

left pair out through gimp to make a ground stitch. Pass right pair back inside gimp to make another honeycomb on left. Make right honeycomb, and with right hand pair W.S. Tw 2, with next right pair. Honeycomb with 2 left hand pairs of this group and honeycomb at centre bottom.

Pass gimp around and cross at centre. Pass new right hand gimp up through 5 pairs and leave centre motif. Now work on left to make left hand tally. The outside left gimp will be vertical. The pair to the right of it will keep passing back and forth through it.

Start by passing this pair to left of gimp. Make ground stitch catch pin and stitch. Pass pair to right through gimp and make 6 ground stitches diagonally to right. Pass gimp through again and make ground stitch. Pass right hand pair back and make 5 ground stitches to right. After tally has been worked, make 1 more ground row and leave.

Make third honeycomb ring next, starting with 2 centre pairs, and after pin on left making W.S. 2 Tw with 2 left hand pairs. Bring gimp round and cross. Pass each gimp through 2 pairs, Tw 2 on each and begin next honeycomb ring at centre. Holes outside gimp are almost horizontal to holes inside. This follows the original Malmesbury sample. The honeycomb ring at bottom left can now be worked followed by a section of footside and ground on the left.

When picot **A1** is reached, bring the pair from that picot back through 2 pairs in whole stitch and leave it. The catch pin and stitch is no longer needed. The next row is made with a ground stitch at the last inside pin-hole. The left pair makes W.S. through 3 pairs. Lay back the centre pair of these 3 pairs and make the next picot, bring the picot pair back in W.S. through 2 pairs, and leave. Make 1 more row. Lay back a second pair from centre of passives, make picot and leave.

Go over to right hand side. Make footside with catch pin and a tally on the third row. Make the fourth row, then the bottom right honeycomb ring, and the bottom centre ring. Cross the gimps at the bottom of this ring, pass them up through 2 pairs and lay them back. The gimps should lie together and the pairs are then twisted; 3 rows on the left can now be completed.

One complete diagonal row can be made, and a tally at the centre bottom on next row. Make last 2 diagonal rows inside gimp. Bring the gimps to centre, cross and pass each up through 2 pairs and lay back. Again, twist 2 on each pair after double gimps. Complete 2 diagonal rows outside the gimp on each side.

After the picot has been made at **A2**, bring that pair back to lie third from edge. Next pair from ground, W.S. out through 3 pairs, lay back centre pair. Make picot, bring that pair back in W.S. to lie third from edge. Repeat down the line. Make sure the threads are tightened up inside each picot. Make the bottom picot with the second pair from left. W.S. out through 1 pair, make picot, W.S. back through 2 pairs. Tie the centre threads, then the next 2 centre threads, and continue until all threads are tied.

Pattern 25:
Finger Motif

Bobbins 20 pairs – Gimp 1 pair

Start in the same manner as the previous pattern.

After the ordinary picot below **F**, hang 1 pair on a temporary pin, and lay it down third from edge. Make a false picot at **G**. With right hand pair make W.S. through 3 pairs. Tw 2, ground stitch. With left hand pair from **G**, W.S. through 1 pair. With third from edge W.S. out through 2 pairs, picot, W.S. back through 3 pairs, Tw 2, ground stitch.

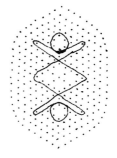

Pricking 25. *Finger Motif*

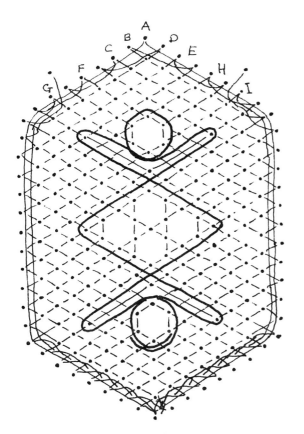

Diagram 25. *Finger Motif*

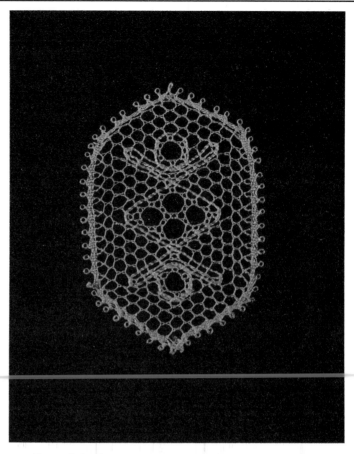

25. *Finger Motif*

Make second row of ground.

With fourth pair from edge (a pair from a ground stitch) make next picot. W.S. through 3 pairs to make last ground stitch of second row.

Remove temorary pin and pull down loop. With this pair make next picot and begin catch pin footside. The right side is worked making false picots at **H** and **I**, adding one pair above **I**.

Refer to Patterns 21 and 22 for working 'fingers'.

Pattern 26:
Small Flower Earrings

Bobbins   16 pairs – Gimps   1 pair

These are made on a smaller grid so a slightly finer thread is used – Mettler 60/2.

Start in the same way as the larger 'hexagon' motif (Pattern 24), with false picots at **A, B, C, D** and **E**. Centre left pair W.S. through 4 pairs to left. Centre right pair through 4 pairs to right. With 2 centre pairs W.S.

With left hand of these W.S. through 2 pairs to left, and with right hand of these W.S. through 2 pairs to right.

Twist 2 on centre pairs and make a ground stitch. Gently pull all threads until tight. Make next ground stitch. With third from left make an ordinary picot and ground stitch.

Hang 1 pair on temporary pin and allow it to fall third from edge. Make false picot at **F** and work right hand pair in W.S. through 3 pairs, and into the ground.

With left hand pair W.S. through 1 pair. With third from edge make an ordinary picot. W.S. through 3 pairs and into the ground.

Pricking 26. *Small Flower Earrings*

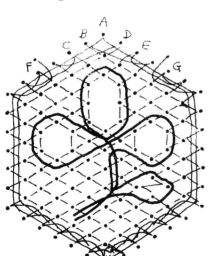

Diagram 26. *Small Flower Earrings*

26. *Small Flower Earrings*

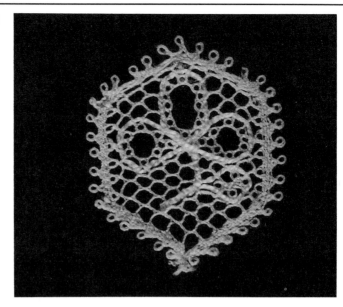

Remove temporary pin and gently pull loop down. Use this pair – third from edge – to make next picot, and begin to make a catch pin stitch at sides.

Reverse for right hand side, i.e. with left hand pair from **E** make a ground stitch. Right hand from **E**, whole stitch through 1 pair. Third from edge makes an ordinary picot then a ground stitch.

Hang 1 pair on a temporary pin and lay it down third from right. Make a false picot at **G**. Left hand makes W.S. through 3 pairs and ground stitch. Right hand pair W.S. through 1 pair. Third from edge makes an ordinary picot. W.S. through 3 pairs and ground stitch.

Remove temporary pin, pull down loop. Make an ordinary picot with this pair and start making catch pin at sides.

The second earring can be made on the same pricking. Rub out the bottom half of the gimp mark and mark it in on the opposite side. If you have trouble following the diagram trace it and turn the tracing over.

Earrings can be obtained from specialist suppliers (see page 117). I used a piece of black Jersey stretch fabric to mount mine, and I found my pin lifter useful to hook the fabric on to the mount.

See diagram 18b for working the little flower.

Pattern 27:
Small Flower Pendant

Bobbins   16 pairs – Gimps   1 pair

This is also made on a smaller grid and uses Mettler 60/2 thread. It fits the tiny pendant which Doreen Campbell sells. Start in the same manner as the earrings.

After the ordinary picot below **F** the picot pair makes W.S. through 3 pairs and ground stitch. Make a second row of ground. Remove temporary pin and pull down the loop. With this pair(third from edge) make the next picot and W.S. back through 3 pairs, including the last pair from the first row of ground. Make a ground stitch at the bottom of the second row.

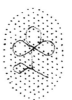

Pricking 27. *Small Flower Pendant*

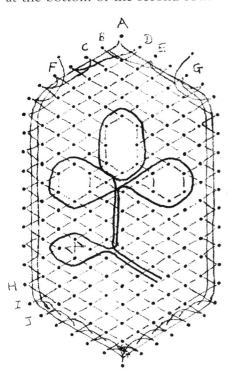

Diagram 27. *Small Flower Pendant*

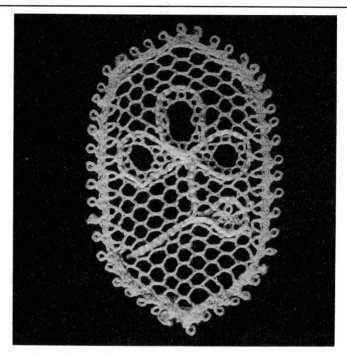

27. *Small Flower Pendant*

With third from edge make an ordinary picot, W.S. through 2 pairs and begin to work a catch pin at the sides.

After the last catch pin and picot at **H**, the picot pair makes W.S. through 3 pairs, including one ground pair. Tw 2 and make a ground stitch at the bottom of the next row.

Third from edge makes the next picot at **I** and returns to third place from edge. The next pair from the ground makes W.S. through 3 pairs. Tw 3. Lay back the centre of the 3 pairs. Make picot **J** and return to third place from the edge. Continue in this way and work the right hand side in reverse until 1 pin-hole is left and there are 6 pairs. With the second pair from left W.S. through 1 pair and make the last picot. W.S. back through 2 pairs. Tie the centre 2 *threads* and lay back. Continue until all pairs are tied.

Leave the last 4 threads long to thread through the backing.

Pattern 28:

Honeycomb Fan and Four Pin Bud Motif

Bobbins *15 pairs – Gimps* *1 pair + 1 single*

Hang 1 pair on each support pin **A-B** (8 pairs). Hang
1 pair each on **C** and **D**. Hang 1 pair gimp between **C**
and **A** and also a single gimp alongside the left hand one
of the pair; this should be fastened tightly to a pin
above the work.

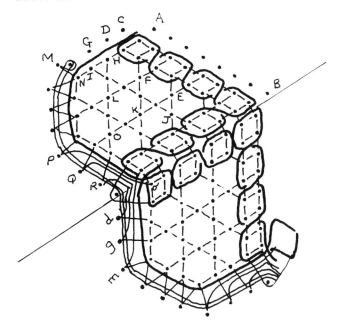

Pricking 28. *Honeycomb Fan
and Four Pin Bud Motif*

Diagram 28. *Honeycomb Fan and Four Pin Bud Motif*

Pass a double gimp on left through the two pairs hanging
from **C** and **D** and pass the right hand of the gimp pair
through 2 pairs to right. Tw 2 on these 4 pairs and make a
4 pin honeycomb ring. Remove the first 4 support pins as
you go along, but leave the one the single gimp is hanging
from.

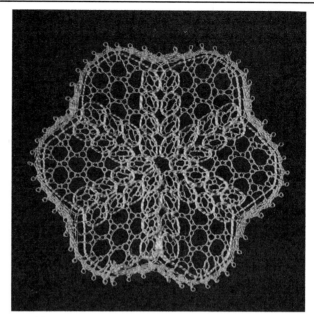

28. *Honeycomb Fan and Four Pin Bud Motif*

*Bring gimp pair through 2 pairs each and cross right over left, pass new right hand up through 2 pairs and also through 2 new pairs from support pins. Tw 2 on each and make second honeycomb ring. Repeat from * until **B** is reached. Remember to remove support pins as you go along.

After the fourth ring bring the gimps to the centre, cross right over left and pass the new left hand one through 3 pairs to left. The third pair will be hanging from the bottom pin of the third ring. Go back to the headside making honeycomb at **E** and **F** as you go.

Hang 1 pair on **D** again and 1 pair on **G**. Pass the single gimp through these 2 pairs, Tw 2 and make honeycomb at **H** and **I** and a long row down to **J**. Another honeycomb ring can be worked, and honeycomb at **K** and **L** on the way back to the headside.

Three pairs are hung on the pin-hole inside **M** which does not appear on subsequent sections. The third pair from left make W.S. through 2 pairs to left. Picot at **M**, W.S. back through 2 pairs, pass inside single gimp and make honeycomb pin **N**. This pair passes in and out along the headside making picots at the edge. The next long row and honeycomb ring can be worked, making honeycomb at **O** on the way back to the headside.

Make the picot and next long row and honeycomb ring. Pass single gimp down through all pairs, twist 2. After picot **P** the picot pair makes W.S. through all pairs and passes through double gimps to make pin-hole **a** in the next section.

After picots **Q** and **R**, the picot pairs make W.S. back through 2 pairs and lie in third place from edge. The left hand pair from the honeycomb ring works out to the valley pin, and the left hand pair from the bottom of the honeycomb ring will be used to make picot **m** in the next section. Picots at **d** and **g** are made with third pair from edge.

At the valley the single gimp is crossed with the left hand one from the bottom of the honeycomb ring, which becomes the new single in the headside.

After the last section carry on with the valley pin and picots **d** and **g** as though you were beginning another section, and as each pair reaches the gimp lay it aside to be sewn in around the gimp when all pins have been worked. The remaining 3 pairs after the last picot are sewn into the beginning of the passives.

Pattern 29:

Bat and Ball Motif

Bobbins   19 pairs – Gimp   1 pair

This motif is not started at an intersection. The join can be hidden more easily by starting at a gimp line.
Therefore start by using the line of pin-holes above the gimp as support pins, and hang 1 pair on each.

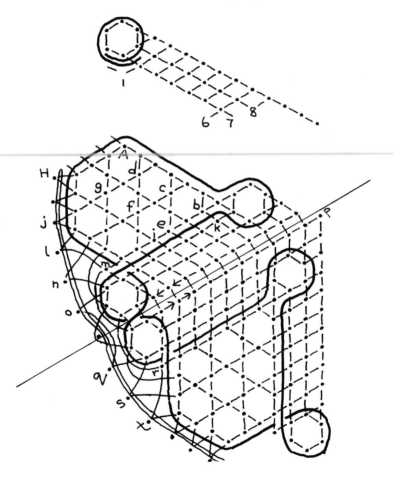

Diagram 29. *Bat and Ball Motif*

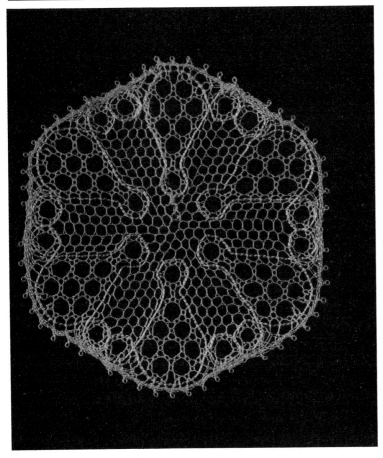

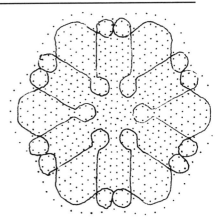

Pricking 29. *Bat and Ball Motif*

29. *Bat and Ball Motif*

Hang the gimp on a temporary pin at **A** and pass the right
hand gimp through 6 pairs. Hang 1 pair on a temporary
pin at the left and pass the left hand gimp through it.
Tw 2 on all pairs.

Make honeycomb stitch with the two left hand pairs
replacing pin **A**, and continue down the line to the right.
Now pass the right hand gimp through 4 more pairs,
supported above the line. Tw 2 on each.

*Honeycomb with the centre 2 pairs and make 2 more
honeycomb stitches to the left, meeting the first line of
honeycomb. Make 1 honeycomb at the right and pass the
right hand pair outside the gimp. ** Hang 1 pair on each of the
2 holes below the intersection and make 2 ground stitches.

Remove all support pins. Pass third from right back inside the gimp and complete the honeycomb ring. Pass the gimp around, Tw 2 on each pair and make 2 more ground stitches to right. On the way back to the headside make up honeycomb stitches at **b**, **c** and **d**.

Hang 3 more pairs on support pins at the left and pass the left hand gimp through them, twist 2 on each and make a line of honeycomb to the left. Remove support pins.

With third and fourth from left, begin a long line of honeycomb stopping at the gimp line. Make up honeycomb stitches at **e**, **f** and **g** on the way back to the headside.

Pass left hand pair outside the gimp. Hang 2 new pairs on a support pin and whole stitch through these, which will remain as the headside passives. Picot at **H** and the picot pair will pass in and out along the top of the headside. A long row can be made to **i**, and a gap row on the way back to the headside. After picot **j**, the last long line can be made and the gimp passed down the line on both sides. At **k** the pairs each side of the pin-hole begin to make ground stitches and this pin holds the gimp up in position. All ground stitches can now be made except the last one.

The pair from picot **1** makes W.S. through 4 pairs. Tw 2, honeycomb at **m**. Cross the gimps and pass the right hand pair from **m** inside the honeycomb ring. Also 2 pairs from the ground at the right pass into the honeycomb ring and this ring can be started. After the 2nd pin-hole on the right, the right hand pair passes outside the gimp to make up the last ground hole and back through the gimp.

The third from left now makes W.S. through 2 pairs to left, picot at **n**, and W.S. through 4 pairs. Pass it inside the gimp to make the second pin-hole, and back out to make picot **o**, and W.S. back to third place from edge. With the fourth from left, W.S. through 1 pair and pass inside the gimp, honeycomb at the third hole and pass back out to the edge. Twist 3 and put up the valley pin and leave. Complete the honeycomb ring.

Pass the gimps around and cross at centre. Fifth from edge, W.S. through 1 pair. Pass inside new left hand gimp. With the valley pair at edge, W.S. through 4 pairs and pass inside the gimp.

Turn the pillow so that the line through the pattern is horizontal.

Pass new right hand gimp through 2 pairs to right. Start the new honeycomb ring with centre 2 pairs. After the second hole on left, the left hand pair passes outside the gimp, and W.S. through 1 pair which is travelling along the outside of the gimp to make honeycomb at **r**.

The third from the left makes picot at **q** and W.S. through 4 pairs. Pass inside gimp to make third honeycomb hole and out again to make picot **s** and back to third from edge.

Complete the honeycomb ring making 1 ground stitch to right. Pass the gimps around and cross. Make honeycomb at **r** with the 2 pairs to left of gimps, and left hand pair goes out to make picot **t**. Pass the right hand pair from **r** inside new left hand gimp to begin a long honeycomb row. With the next two pairs to left of gimp Tw 2 and pass inside gimp.

To the right of the honeycomb ring make 1 complete row of ground, adding 1 pair at centre, at **p**. Make two more rows to the gimp line.

Pass right hand through 6 pairs, Tw 2 on each, and make up long honeycomb line. Pass the same gimp through 4 more pairs to right and begin the honeycomb ring with the centre 2 pairs. Repeat from * to **.

After the last complete section, 1 more honeycomb ring is made and 1 line of ground to the centre, then 2 more lines to gimp.

Take great care in joining. Two pairs are sewn into **1** and **8**, and nothing into the hole between **6** and **7**. Honeycomb is made at **r** and picots are made at **s** and **t**, and the pairs from these picots, and from the pin-hole adjacent to **q** are sewn into the honeycomb pin-holes to the left of **1**. The 2 remaining passive pairs are sewn into the beginning of the headside passives.

Pattern 30:
Chain and Chevron Motif

Bobbins   16 pairs – Gimps   1 pair

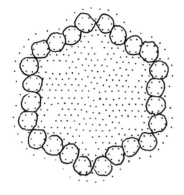

Pricking 30. *Chain and Chevron Motif*

Hang the gimp on a temporary pin at **A**. Hang 2 pairs to the left. Hang 10 pairs to the right on temporary pins above the intersection. Pass gimps to right and left through 2 pairs each, Tw 2.

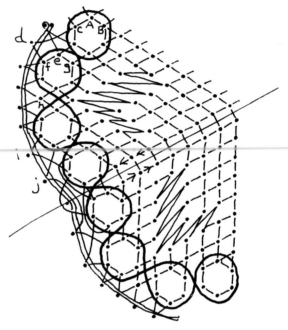

Diagram 30. *Chain and Chevron Motif*

*Begin the honeycomb ring with centre 2 pairs replacing pin **A**. After **B**, the right hand pair goes out through the gimp to make the first ground stitch and back to continue the honeycomb ring. The left hand pair from **C** passes outside the gimp.

Hang 2 pairs on a temporary pin at the left, and 2 pairs outside them, splayed. Make a false picot with these two

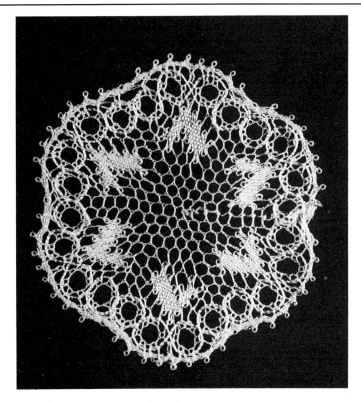

30. *Chain and Chevron Motif*

pairs and with each pair W.S. through 2 pairs. With left hand from **C**, W.S. to left through 4 pairs. Twist 3, make picot at **d**.

With fifth from left, Tw 2, and pass inside the gimp to continue honeycomb ring which can be completed. Pass gimps around and cross them at the centre. Pass new left hand gimp up through 2 pairs. With fourth from edge Tw 2, and pass inside the gimp. With picot pair from **d**, W.S. through 2 pairs. Tw 2, pass inside gimp.

Before beginning the second honeycomb ring, make a line of ground stitch to the centre with all pairs hanging from support pins, and a short line of ground stitch to the right of the first honeycomb ring.

Start the second honeycomb ring with the centre 2 pairs of the 4 pairs inside gimps. The left hand from **f** will go out to make the next picot and back to continue the honeycomb ring. The right hand from **g** passes the gimp to make a ground stitch, and back in to continue the honeycomb ring which can be completed. Pass the gimps around and cross at centre, make another picot and a honeycomb stitch at the left of the crossed gimps, and from it the left hand pair goes out to make another picot and W.S. back through 2 pairs. Pass the third and fourth pairs through left hand gimp.

Begin the top of the W.S. chevron with the centre 2 pairs, then bring in a pair from the right first, then from the left. Bring one more from the right, then continue bringing in pairs from the left and leaving out at right. Stop at the widest point of the chevron. Three pairs from right of chevron are twisted twice and begin the centre ground.

The bottom of the chevron can be completed leaving out pairs on left and bringing in pairs from the right. Note that this is an irregular chevron. The bottom half is narrower than the top. One row of ground holes remains to be worked above the intersection when the chevron is complete.

Pairs from the left of the chevron are twisted twice. The new right hand gimp is passed through 2 pairs to right. Begin the new honeycomb ring with the centre 2 pairs inside gimps.

After the first right hole, the right hand pair passes outside the gimp to start a row of ground stitch. The pair passes back inside the gimp to continue the honeycomb ring.

After the first left hole, the left hand pair passes out to make a picot and back to continue the honeycomb ring, which can be completed.

Bring the gimps round and cross them at centre. Pass the new right hand gimp through 4 pairs to the right. Tw 2 on each and begin the last honeycomb ring with the centre 2 pairs. After the first right hole, the right hand pair passes outside the gimp to make the last ground stitch and back to continue the honeycomb ring. After the first left hole, pass the left hand pair outside the gimp, Tw 2, and it then travels alongside the gimp to begin the next section.

With the third from left, W.S. out through 2 pairs, picot **i**, W.S. back through 4 pairs, pass inside gimp to work second left hole in honeycomb ring, then out through gimp and W.S. through 1 pair. Complete ring and pass gimps around. Cross at centre.

With the third from left, W.S. out through 2 pairs to make picot **j**, and W.S. back to third place. With the fourth from left W.S. out through 3 pairs, Tw 3, and put up valley pin.

The bottom left pair from honeycomb ring will travel with gimp to work second left hole in the next honeycomb ring. Pass the new right hand gimp through 2 pairs to right. With fifth pair from left, W.S. through 1 pair to right, Tw 2, pass inside gimp.

With the valley pair at left, W.S. through 4 pairs, Tw 2 and pass inside the gimp. Turn the pillow and start the next section with the centre 2 pairs inside the gimp.

Begin again at *.

After the last honeycomb ring, when the gimps are crossed, each can be passed up through pairs to right and left so that the double gimps lie together with no twists between. They can then be laid back.

Sew two pairs into **A**, 1 into **C** and the remaining 4 pairs into the passive starting loops.

Reference Information

Bibliography:
Sources of Information for Part One

Books

E. Lipson, *Economic History of England*, A & C Black, 1956

Malmesbury schoolchildren, *Man in Malmesbury*, Malmesbury School, 1973

Palliser, Mrs Bury, *A History of Lace*, Tower Books, Detroit, reprinted 1976

Victoria County History of Wiltshire, Vol VII, Oxford University Press

Waylen, James, *History of Marlborough*, 1853

Other sources

Huguenot Society Quarto Series Vols XX, XLIX

Privy Council Registers P.C. 2/64.17.480

Royal Archives, Windsor Castle

The Salisbury and Winchester Journal, 1841

Wiltshire Times, 27 January 1912

Suppliers and sources of information

General Suppliers

United Kingdom

Alby Lace Museum
Cromer Road
Alby
Norfolk
NR11 7QE

Busy Bobbins
Unit 7
Scarrots Lane
Newport
Isle of Wight
PO30 1JD

Chosen Crafts Centre
46 Winchcombe Street
Cheltenham
Gloucestershire
GL52 2ND

Jo Firth
Lace Marketing & Needlecraft
  Supplies
58 Kent Crescent
Lowtown
Pudsey
West Yorkshire
LS28 9EB

J. & J. Ford
October Hill
Upper Way
Upper Longdon
Rugeley
Staffordshire
WS15 1QB

Framecraft
83 Hampstead Road
Handsworth Wood
Birmingham
B2 1JA

Doreen Gill
14 Barnfield Road
Petersfield
Hampshire
GU31 4DQ

R. Gravestock
Highwood
Crews Hill
Alfrick
Worcestershire
WR6 5HF

The Handicraft Shop
47 Northgate
Canterbury
Kent
CT1 1BE

Frank Herring & Sons
27 High West Street
Dorchester
Dorset
DT1 1UP

Honiton Lace Shop
44 High Street
Honiton
Devon

D. J. Hornsby
149 High Street
Burton Latimer
Kettering
Northamptonshire
NN15 5RL

also at:
25 Manwood Avenue
Canterbury
Kent
CT2 7AH

Frances Iles
73 High Street
Rochester
Kent
ME1 1LX

Jane's Pincushions
Unit 4
Taverham Crafts
Taverham Nursery Centre
Fir Covert Road
Taverham
Norwich
NR8 6HT

Loricraft
19 Peregrine Way
Grove
Wantage
Oxfordshire

Needlestyle
5 The Woolmead
Farnham
Surrey
GU9 7TX

Needlestyle
24–26 West Street
Alresford
Hampshire

Needlework
Ann Bartlee
Bucklers Farm
Coggeshall
Essex
CO6 1SB

Needle and Thread
80 High Street
Horsell
Woking
Surrey
GU21 4SZ

The Needlewoman
21 Needless Alley
off New Street
Birmingham
B2 5AE

T. Parker
124 Corhampton Road
Boscombe East
Bournemouth
Dorset
BH6 5NZ

Jane Playford
North Lodge
Church Close
West Runton
Norfolk
NR27 9QY

Redburn Crafts
Squires Garden Centre
Halliford Road
Upper Halliford
Shepperton
Middlesex
TW17 8RU

Christine Riley
53 Barclay Street
Stonehaven
Kincardineshire
Scotland

Peter & Beverley Scarlett
Strupak
Hill Head
Cold Wells
Ellon
Grampian
Scotland

Ken & Pat Schultz
134 Wisbech Road
Thornley
Peterborough

J. S. Sear
Lacecraft Supplies
8 Hill View
Sherrington
Buckinghamshire
MK16 9NY

Sebalace
Waterloo Mills
Howden Road
Silsden
West Yorkshire
BD2 0NA

A. Sells
49 Pedley Lane
Clifton
Shefford
Bedfordshire

Shireburn Lace
Finkle Court
Finkle Hill
Sherburn in Elmet
North Yorkshire
LS25 6EB

SMP
4 Garners Close
Chalfont St Peter
Buckinghamshire
SL9 0HB

Southern Handicrafts
20 Kensington Gardens
Brighton
Sussex
BN1 4AC

Spangles
Carole Morris
Burwell
Cambridgeshire
CB5 0ED

Stitches
Dovehouse Shopping Parade
Warwick Road
Olton
Solihull
West Midlands

Teazle Embroideries
35 Boothferry Road
Hull
North Humberside

Valley House Craft Studios
Ruston
Scarborough
North Yorkshire

George Walker
The Corner Shop
Rickinghall
Diss
Norfolk

West End Lace Supplies
Ravensworth Court Road
Mortimer West End
Reading
Berkshire
RG7 3UD

George White Lacemakers'
  Supplies
40 Heath Drive
Boston Spa
West Yorkshire
L23 6PB

Bobbins

A. R. Archer
The Poplars
Shetland
near Stowmarket
Suffolk
IP14 3DE

T. Brown
Temple Lane Cottage
Littledean
Cinderford
Gloucestershire

Chrisken Bobbins
26 Cedar Drive
Kingsclere
Buckinghamshire
RG15 8TD

Malcolm J. Fielding
2 Northern Terrace
Moss Lane
Silverdale
Lancashire
LA5 0ST

Richard Gravestock
Highwood
Crews Hill, Alfrick
Worcestershire
WR6 5HF

Larkfield Crafts
Hilary Rickitts
4 Island Cottages
Mapledurwell
Basingstoke
Hampshire
RG25 2LU

Loricraft
19 Peregrine Way
Grove
Wantage
Oxfordshire

T. Parker
124 Corhampton Road
Boscombe East
Bournemouth
Dorset
BH6 5NZ

Bryan Phillips
Pantglas
Cellan
Lampeter
Dyfed
SA48 8JD

D. H. Shaw
47 Lamor Crescent
Thrushcroft
Rotherham
South Yorkshire
S66 9QD

Sizelands
1 Highfield Road
Winslow
Buckinghamshire
MK10 3QU

Christine & David Springett
21 Hillmorton Road
Rugby
Warwickshire
CV22 5DF

Richard Viney
Unit 7
Port Royal Street
Southsea
Hampshire
PO5 3UD

West End Lace Suppliers
Ravensworth Court Road
Mortimer West End
Reading
Berkshire
RG7 3UD

Gemstones and jewellery findings

Gaycharm Ltd (mail order)
168 Chadwell Heath Road
Romford
Essex
RM6 6HT

Lace pillows

Newnham Lace Equipment
15 Marlowe Close
Basingstoke
Hampshire
RG24 9DD

Books

Christopher Williams
19 Morrison Avenue
Parkstone
Poole
Dorset
BH17 4AD

Silk embroidery and lace thread

E. & J. Piper
Silverlea
Flax Lane
Glemsford
Suffolk
CO10 7RS

Silk weaving yarn

Hilary Chetwynd
Kipping Cottage
Cheriton
Alresford
Hampshire
SO24 0PW

Frames and mounts

Doreen Campbell
Highcliff
Bremilsham Road
Malmesbury
Wiltshire
SN16 0DQ

Matt coloured transparent adhesive film

Heffers Graphic Shop
26 King Street
Cambridge
CB1 1LN

Linen by the metre (yard) and made up articles of church linen

Mary Collins
Church Furnishings
St Andrews Hall
Humber Doucy Lane
Ipswich
Suffolk
IP4 3BP

Hayes & Finch
Head Office & Factory
Hanson Road
Aintree
Liverpool
L9 9BP

United States of America

Arbor House
22 Arbor Lane
Roslyn Hights
NY 11577

Baltazor Inc.
3262 Severn Avenue
Metairie
LA 7002

Beggars' Lace
P.O. Box 17263
Denver
Colorado 80217

Berga Ullman Inc.
P.O. Box 918
North Adams
Massachusetts 01247

Frederick J. Fawcett
129 South Street
Boston
Massachusetts 02130

Frivolité
15526 Densmore N.
Seattle
Washington 98113

Happy Hands
3007 S. W. Marshall
Pendleton
Oregon 97180

International Old Lacers
P.O. Box 1029
Westminster
Colorado 80030

Lace Place de Belgique
800 S. W. 17th Street
Boca Raton
FL 33432

Lacis
2150 Stuart Street
Berkeley
California 9470

Robin's Bobbins
RTL Box 1736
Mineral Bluff
Georgia 30559

Robin and Russ
Handweavers
533 North Adams Street
McMinnvills
Oregon 97128

Some Place
2990 Adline Street
Berkeley
California 94703

Osma G. Todd Studio
319 Mendoza Avenue
Coral Gables
Florida 33134

The Unique And Art Lace
  Cleaners
5926 Delman Boulevard
St Louis
Missouri 63112

Van Scriver Bobbin Lace
130 Cascadilla Park
Ithaca
New York 14850

The World in Stitches
82 South Street
Milford
N.H. 03055

Australia

Dentelles Lace Supplies
3 Narrak Close
Jindalee
Queensland 4074

The Lacemaker
94 Fordham Avenue
Hartwell
Victoria 3124

Spindle and Loom
Arcade 83
Longueville Road
Lane Cove
NSW 2066

Tulis Crafts
201 Avoca Street
Randwick
NSW 2031

Belgium

't Handwekhuisje
Katelijnestraat 23
8000 Bruges

Kantcentrum
Balstraat 14
8000 Bruges

Manufacture Belge de Dentelle
6 Galerie de la Reine
Galeries Royales St Hubert
1000 Bruxelles

Orchidée
Mariastraat 18
8000 Bruges

Ann Thys
't Apostelientje
Balstraat 11
8000 Bruges

France

Centre d'Initiations à la
    Dentelle du Puy
2 Rue Duguesclin
43000 Le Puy en Velay

A L'Econome
Anne-Marie Deydier
Ecole de Dentelle aux Fuseaux
10 rue Paul Chenavard
69001 Lyon

Rugier and Plé
13–15 bd des Filles de Calvaire
75003 Paris

West Germany

Der Fenster Laden
Berliner Str. 8
D 6483 Bad Soden
Salmünster

P.P. Hempel
Ortolanweg 34
1000 Berlin 47

Heikona De Ruijter
Kleoppelgrosshandel
Langer Steinweg 38
D4933 Blomberg

Holland

Blokker's Boektiek
Bronsteeweg 4/4a
2101 AC Heemstede

Theo Brejaat
Postbus 5199
3008 AD Rotterdam

Magazijn *De Vlijt*
Lijnmarkt 48
Utrecht

Switzerland

Fadehax
Inh. Irene Solca
4105 Biel-Benken
Basel

New Zealand

Peter McLeavey
P.O. Box 69.007
Auckland 8

Sources of information

The Lace Guild
The Hollies
53 Audnam
Stourbridge
West Midlands
DY8 4AE

The Lace Society
Linwood
Stratford Road
Oversley
Alcester
Warwickshire
BY9 6PG

The British College of Lace
21 Hillmorton Road
Rugby
Warwickshire
CV22 5DF

The English Lace School
Oak House
Church Stile
Woodbury
Nr Exeter
Devon

International Old Lacers
President
Gunvor Jorgensen
366 Bradley Avenue
Northvale
NJ 076647
United States

Ring of Tatters
Mrs C. Appleton
Nonesuch
5 Ryeland Road
Ellerby
Saltburn by Sea
Cleveland
TS13 5LP

United Kingdom Director of
International Old Lacers
S. Hurst
4 Dollius Road
London
N3 1RG

Books

*The following are stockists of
the complete Batsford/Dryad Press range:*

Avon
Bridge Bookshop
7 Bridge Street
Bath
BA2 4AS

Waterstone & Co.
4–5 Milsom Street
Bath
BA1 1DA

Bedfordshire
Arthur Sells
Lane Cove
49 Pedley Lane
Clifton
Sefford
SG17 5QT

Berkshire
West End Lace Supplies
Ravensworth Court Road
Mortimer West End
Reading
RG7 3UD

Buckinghamshire
J. S. Sear Lacecraft Supplies
8 Hill View
Sherringham
MK16 9NY

Cambridgeshire
Dillons the Bookstore
Sydney Street
Cambridge

Cheshire
Lyn Turner
Church Meadow Crafts
15 Carisbrook Drive
Winsford
Cheshire

Devon
Creative Crafts & Needlework
18 High Street
Totnes
TQ9 5NP

Honiton Lace Shop
44 High Street
Honiton
EX14 8PJ

Dorset
F. Herring & Sons
High West Street
Dorchester
DT1 1UP

Tim Parker (mail order)
124 Corhampton Road
Boscombe East
Bournemouth
BH6 5NL

Durham
Lacemaid
6, 10 & 15 Stoneybeck
Bishop Middleham
County Durham
DL17 9BL

Gloucestershire
Southgate Handicrafts
68 Southgate Street
Gloucester
GL1 1TX

Waterstone & Co.
89–90 The Promenade
Cheltenham
GL50 1NB

Hampshire
Creative Crafts
11 The Square
Winchester
SO23 9ES

Doreen Gill
14 Barnfield Road
Petersfield
GU31 4DR

Larkfield Crafts
4 Island Cottages
Mapledurwell
Basingstoke
RG23 2LU

Needlestyle
24–26 West Street
Alresford

Ruskins
27 Bell Street
Romsey

Isle of Wight
Busy Bobbins
Unit 7
Scarrots Lane
Newport
PO30 1JD

Kent
The Handicraft Shop
47 Northgate
Canterbury

Frances Iles
73 High Street
Rochester
ME1 1LX

Lincolnshire
Rippingale Lace
Barn Farm House
off Station Road
Rippingdale Bourne

London
Foyles
119 Charing Cross Road
WC2H 0EB

Hatchards
187 Piccadilly
W1

Middlesex
Redburn Crafts
Squires Garden Centre
Halliford Road
Upper Halliford
Shepperton
TW17 8RU

Norfolk
Alby Lace Museum
Cromer Road
Alby
nr Aylsham
NR11 7QE

Jane's Pincushions
Taverham Craft Unit 4
Taverham Nursery Centre
Fir Covert Road
Taverham
Norwich
NR8 6HT

Waterstone & Co.
30 London Street
Norwich
NR2 1LD

Northamptonshire
D. J. Hornsby
149 High Street
Burton Latimer
Kettering
NN15 5RL

Oxfordshire
Loricraft
19 Peregrine Way
Grove
Wantage

Scotland
Embroidery Shop
51 Withain Street
Edinburgh
Lothian
EH3 7LW

Beverley Scarlett
Strupak
Hillhead
Coldwells
Ellon
Aberdeenshire

Waterstone & Co.
236 Union Street
Aberdeen
AB1 1TN

Surrey
Needlestyle
5 The Woolmead
Farnham
GU9 1TN

Sussex
Southern Handicrafts
20 Kensington Gardens
Brighton
BN1 4AL

Warwickshire
Christine & David Springett
21 Hillmorton Road
Rugby
CV22 6DF

North Yorkshire
Shireburn Lace
Finkel Court
Finkel Hill
Leeds
LS25 6EA

Valley House Craft Studios
Ruston
Scarborough

West Midlands
Needlewoman
Needles Alley
off New Street
Birmingham

West Yorkshire
Sebalace
Waterloo Mill
Howden Road
Silsden
BD20 0HA

George White Lacemaking
   Supplies
40 Heath Drive
Boston Spa
LS23 6PB

Jo Firth
58 Kent Crescent
Lowtown
Pudsey
Leeds LS28 9EB

Index

George White Lacemaking
  Supplies
40 Heath Drive
Boston Spa
LS23 6PB

Jo Firth
58 Kent Crescent
Lowtown
Pudsey
Leeds LS28 9EB